WHAT THE BIBLE SAYS ABOUT YOUR FUTURE

WHAT THE BIBLE SAYS ABOUT YOUR FUTURE

BIBLICAL PROPHECIES
FOR EVERY BELIEVER

DR. JOHN F. WALVOORD

David C Cook®
transforming lives together

WHAT THE BIBLE SAYS ABOUT YOUR FUTURE
Published by David C Cook
4050 Lee Vance Drive
Colorado Springs, CO 80918 U.S.A.

David C Cook U.K., Kingsway Communications
Eastbourne, East Sussex BN23 6NT, England

The graphic circle C logo is a registered trademark of David C Cook.

The website addresses recommended throughout this book are offered as a
resource to you. These websites are not intended in any way to be or imply an
endorsement on the part of David C Cook, nor do we vouch for their content.

Unless otherwise noted, all Scripture quotations are taken from the Holy
Bible, NEW INTERNATIONAL VERSION®, NIV®. Copyright © 1973,
2011 by Biblica, Inc.® Used by permission. All rights reserved worldwide.
NEW INTERNATIONAL VERSION® and NIV® are registered trademarks
of Biblica, Inc. Use of either trademark for the offering of goods or services
requires the prior written consent of Biblica, Inc. Scripture quotations
marked ESV are taken from the ESV® Bible (The Holy Bible, English
Standard Version®), copyright © 2001 by Crossway, a publishing ministry
of Good News Publishers. Used by permission. All rights reserved.

LCCN 2016959764
ISBN 978-1-4347-1064-2
eISBN 978-1-4347-1155-7

The Team: Tim Peterson, Amy Konyndyk, Nick Lee,
Cara Iverson, Helen Macdonald, Susan Murdock
Cover Design: Jon Middel
Cover Photo: Getty Images

Printed in the United States of America
First Edition 2017

1 2 3 4 5 6 7 8 9 10

012717

CONTENTS

NOTE FROM THE PUBLISHER

God's Grace Guarantees a Fabulous Future

The renowned author C. S. Lewis once commented, "The future is something which everyone reaches at the rate of sixty minutes an hour, whatever he does, whoever he is."

It's true that each person on earth is moving steadily and unceasingly into the future. It's also true that nearly everyone spends considerable time and energy wondering what the future holds. Some look forward with excitement, some with anxiety. Some fear the unknown, while others are motivated by it.

Many people don't just speculate about the future; they also actively try to ascertain details about it. Sadly, countless people seek answers from psychics, fortune-tellers, horoscopes, astrological signs, and so on. An entire industry exists, generating billions of dollars, on the promise that "experts" can tell people in detail how their lives will unfold.

The good news is that there is a much more reliable source of information about the future. God speaks to us through His Word, and within those pages we find clear answers about the shape our lives will take and the way our paths forward will open up. The Bible does not provide details about our individual lives, such as what vocations we will pursue, where we will live, and when we will die. But Scripture does paint a picture of life in broad strokes and, more important, offers a vivid portrait of what our lives will be like when our days on earth end.

God, the Creator of all, has chosen to reveal an amazing amount of information about the future—the world's future and every person's future. For those who claim His Son as Savior, looking ahead need not be fearful or worrisome. Why? Because Scripture is full of assurances that your heavenly Father will provide for you and protect you: "'I know the plans I have for you,' declares the LORD, 'plans to prosper you and not to harm you, plans to give you hope and a future'" (Jer. 29:11).

Scripture does not promise that Christ followers will be exempt from hardships and heartaches. Indeed, the biblical writers tell us that human existence is sure to bring trials and tribulations and that Christians can expect times of persecution (2 Thess. 1:4). If this makes your future seem daunting, cling to the fact that any short-term adversity will pale in comparison to the long-term joy that's in store for you. According to the apostle Paul, "Our light and momentary troubles are achieving for us an eternal glory that far outweighs them all" (2 Cor. 4:17).

In the pages that follow, we'll provide an array of scriptures that, when pieced together, form a mosaic depicting the beautiful future that awaits you. As much as possible, we will allow Scripture to speak for itself when foretelling what your future holds. We have included commentary on many passages to provide context and to clarify terms and references that might be unfamiliar to modern readers. Because the Bible contains hundreds of promises to God's children, we'll explore many of the assurances that directly relate to your life here and beyond. We'll also see that how we live moment by moment, day by day, significantly influences the quality of our lives on earth and the rewards that await us in heaven.

It is our prayer that this book will serve as an open door for God to speak to your heart and mind regarding your future. Most of all, may you draw courage and comfort in knowing that the God who created everything cares deeply about you, now and forever.

FROM THIS POINT FORWARD

A Timeline of the Believer's Life

Each of God's children is unique—a creation completely distinct from any other throughout history. Our loving Creator has designed every individual to be "one of a kind"—a singular blend of talents, tendencies, and personality traits. Still, there are some milestones that all believers will experience as members of God's family.

1. FALLENNESS

Since the fall of mankind, each and every person has been born with sin in his heart. This means that we are born into a broken relationship with God. Psalm 51:5 puts it this way: "Surely I was sinful at birth, sinful from the time my mother conceived me."

God, in His great love and compassion, did not desire for people to remain at odds with Him. Over and over again, He extended His hand to the people of Israel, attempting to restore relationship with them. Yet there was no sacrifice great enough to wash away their sins for all time. God had a solution in mind, and it would come at the cost of the ultimate sacrifice.

Romans 6 describes the great penalty of sin—and God's even greater power:

> When you were slaves to sin, you were free from the control of righteousness. What benefit did you reap at that time from the things you are now ashamed of? Those things result in death! But now that you have been set free from sin and have become slaves of God, the benefit you reap leads to holiness, and the result is eternal life. For the wages of sin is death, but the gift of God is eternal life in Christ Jesus our Lord. (vv. 20–23)

2. REPENTANCE

One of the most pivotal moments in a person's life is when he decides to turn away from sin and seek God's path instead. This rejection of the former ways of life is necessary for a person to be ready for a lifetime of submission to our Savior, Jesus Christ.

The apostle Paul said, "I have declared to both Jews and Greeks that they must turn to God in repentance and have faith in our

Lord Jesus" (Acts 20:21). Later, he wrote, "Godly sorrow brings repentance that leads to salvation and leaves no regret, but worldly sorrow brings death" (2 Cor. 7:10). Without true repentance, faith is not possible. Dwelling in sin is incompatible with living a life of faithfulness. It is only after we have turned away from our sinful selves and declared that God's ways are right that we are ready to be welcomed into His family.

3. BAPTISM

There is some debate among Christians about when and how baptism should occur. What is clear is that baptism is a significant event in the life of a believer, marking the rejection of sin and the declaration of rebirth in Christ.

In Acts 2:38, Peter proclaimed, "Repent and be baptized, every one of you, in the name of Jesus Christ for the forgiveness of your sins. And you will receive the gift of the Holy Spirit."

During baptism, the Holy Spirit fills the believer. But what happens next? How does baptism affect the rest of a believer's life? Scripture describes the many roles of the Holy Spirit, but it's clear that the primary function of the Holy Spirit is to enable a believer to live a new life, characterized by purity and Christlikeness.

The apostle Paul provides this insight:

> What shall we say, then? Shall we go on sinning
> so that grace may increase? By no means! We are
> those who have died to sin; how can we live in it

any longer? Or don't you know that all of us who were baptized into Christ Jesus were baptized into his death? We were therefore buried with him through baptism into death in order that, just as Christ was raised from the dead through the glory of the Father, we too may live a new life. (Rom. 6:1–4)

Thankfully, our sinful nature, which is spiritually toxic and leads to everlasting death, is washed away through baptism.

4. THE JOURNEY

The specifics of your life story—the highs and lows, sorrows and joys—will be as wonderful and mysterious as the Author of life Himself. No one else will ever have your exact story. But there are some themes that others will also share: loss, restoration, joy, and grief, to name a few. As the author of Ecclesiastes wisely observed, life will include many ups and downs, twists and turns:

> There is a time for everything,
>> and a season for every activity under the
>>> heavens:
>
>> a time to be born and a time to die,
>> a time to plant and a time to uproot,
>> a time to kill and a time to heal,

> a time to tear down and a time to build,
>
> a time to weep and a time to laugh,
>
> a time to mourn and a time to dance,
>
> a time to scatter stones and a time to
> > gather them,
>
> a time to embrace and a time to refrain
> > from embracing,
>
> a time to search and a time to give up,
>
> a time to keep and a time to throw away,
>
> a time to tear and a time to mend,
>
> a time to be silent and a time to speak,
>
> a time to love and a time to hate,
>
> a time for war and a time for peace. (3:1–8)

Scripture gives the assurance that through it all God will always be faithful, a trustworthy Father through all the experiences we encounter. The Holy Spirit living within us will supply wisdom and comfort. Here is an overview of what you can anticipate experiencing over the course of your lifetime.

TRIALS

Times of adversity and difficulty are inevitable in life, and these come in many forms; job loss, failing health, financial hardship, and strained relationships are just a few of the ways we can be tried and tested. Trials are a necessary part of strengthening our faith. The ultimate goal is to produce a trust in Jesus so strong that it can withstand any earthly difficulty. A faith like this will help us stand firm in life as we prepare for eternity with Him.

The apostle Peter explained the value of earthly afflictions and struggles:

> In this you rejoice, though now for a little while, if necessary, you have been grieved by various trials, so that the tested genuineness of your faith—more precious than gold that perishes though it is tested by fire—may be found to result in praise and glory and honor at the revelation of Jesus Christ. Though you have not seen him, you love him. Though you do not now see him, you believe in him and rejoice with joy that is inexpressible and filled with glory, obtaining the outcome of your faith, the salvation of your souls. (1 Pet. 1:6–9 ESV)

During times of hardship, it can be easy to lose sight of God's purpose for our lives. After all, we tend to believe that when things are going well, God must be pleased with us. By extension, if times are hard, it must be true that He is displeased. But Scripture actually refutes this line of thinking and often asserts just the opposite. As Paul assured us,

> We rejoice in hope of the glory of God. Not only that, but we rejoice in our sufferings, knowing

that suffering produces endurance, and endurance produces character, and character produces hope, and hope does not put us to shame, because God's love has been poured into our hearts through the Holy Spirit who has been given to us. (Rom. 5:2–5 ESV)

When viewed through this lens, it becomes clear that Jesus has redeemed even our sufferings. Our trials are not wasted; rather, they cultivate hopefulness in our hearts. Not only that, but they lead to another valuable aspect of the Christian life: transformation.

TRANSFORMATION

Baptism is a onetime event in the Christian's life, but repentance is an ongoing practice we must adopt for the rest of our lives. Repentance keeps our hearts soft to the teachings of God through His Word, as well as to the guidance of the Holy Spirit. Confessing our sins to one another and to God opens the door for the transformation of our hearts and minds. As Paul astutely described in his letter to the Colossians,

Put to death, therefore, whatever belongs to your earthly nature: sexual immorality, impurity, lust, evil desires and greed, which is idolatry. Because of these, the wrath of God is coming. You used to walk in these ways, in the life you once lived.

> But now you must also rid yourselves of all such
> things as these: anger, rage, malice, slander, and
> filthy language from your lips. Do not lie to each
> other, since you have taken off your old self with
> its practices and have put on the new self, which
> is being renewed in knowledge in the image of its
> Creator. (Col. 3:5–10)

Renewal in the knowledge of God is the mark of a true believer. You can count on the Holy Spirit transforming you into a better likeness of Christ throughout your life. He will use every circumstance in your life to draw you closer to Jesus. Through this astounding work, others will be able to see Jesus clearly through your life.

PERSECUTION

Again and again throughout Scripture, we see evidence that when a believer models his life after Jesus's teachings, persecution follows close behind. Paul put it plainly in his letter to Timothy, saying, "Everyone who wants to live a godly life in Christ Jesus will be persecuted" (2 Tim. 3:12).

What is persecution, exactly? And how does it differ from other hardships? Peter describes persecution as a particular kind of "fiery trial." Rather than being caught off guard, Peter urges us to expect these types of tribulations:

Beloved, do not be surprised at the fiery trial
when it comes upon you to test you, as though
something strange were happening to you. But
rejoice insofar as you share Christ's sufferings,
that you may also rejoice and be glad when
his glory is revealed. If you are insulted for
the name of Christ, you are blessed, because
the Spirit of glory and of God rests upon you.
(1 Pet. 4:12–14 ESV)

In the Sermon on the Mount, Jesus described persecution as
suffering for the sake of righteousness: "Blessed are those who are
persecuted because of righteousness, for theirs is the kingdom of
heaven" (Matt. 5:10).

The apostle Paul explained that his sufferings had the effect of
advancing the message of the gospel:

I want you to know, brothers and sisters, that
what has happened to me has actually served to
advance the gospel. As a result, it has become
clear throughout the whole palace guard and to
everyone else that I am in chains for Christ. And
because of my chains, most of the brothers and
sisters have become confident in the Lord and dare
all the more to proclaim the gospel without fear.
(Phil. 1:12–14)

As we can see from these examples and others in Scripture, persecution is a holy suffering specifically for the sake of Jesus Christ. We are not left in the dark on the issue of persecution; we know that at some point in our lives, we will experience unjust suffering because of our allegiance to Christ. How should we respond to such treatment? Paul detailed his response in his letter to the church at Corinth: "For Christ's sake, I delight in weaknesses, in insults, in hardships, in persecutions, in difficulties. For when I am weak, then I am strong" (2 Cor. 12:10).

When you experience intense suffering, are you inclined to rejoice? Do you take delight in knowing that you are enduring hardship for the sake of your faith? Or do you, like so many people, fall into despair? Passages such as these remind us that God's economy is different from man's. He values humility, sacrifice, and obedience, and He will empower you to endure every trial that comes your way.

LIVING OUT THE WORD

One unmistakable mark of a transformed and true believer is that he lives in a way that is consistent with God's values. Simply put, a true believer should strive to "walk the walk." As James, brother and follower of Jesus, succinctly wrote,

> Be doers of the word, and not hearers only,
> deceiving yourselves. For if anyone is a hearer
> of the word and not a doer, he is like a man

who looks intently at his natural face in a mirror. For he looks at himself and goes away and at once forgets what he was like. But the one who looks into the perfect law, the law of liberty, and perseveres, being no hearer who forgets but a doer who acts, he will be blessed in his doing.

If anyone thinks he is religious and does not bridle his tongue but deceives his heart, this person's religion is worthless. (1:22–26 ESV)

God has placed you in your family, neighborhood, church, and place of employment for a specific reason. No detail has been overlooked. He desires for you to complete the "good works, which God prepared in advance" for you to do (Eph. 2:10). Your life will be filled with opportunities to bless, encourage, support, and challenge others. The best part is that you will not be left to your own devices; the Holy Spirit will fill and empower you to do these tasks so you may be a reflection of Jesus Christ.

FAMILY REUNION

None of us knows how many days we will be given on this earth. Thankfully, God Himself has prearranged all the details. He knew exactly when we would be born and knows when our lives will come to an end. It's not uncommon for people to worry about death. Even the most faithful believers can feel unease about the idea of dying. But Jesus helps us maintain a proper perspective: "Do not be afraid of those who kill the body but cannot kill the soul. Rather, be afraid of the One who can destroy both soul and body in hell" (Matt. 10:28).

Whether you are alive to witness the coming of Jesus or your life ends naturally, you can take comfort in the knowledge that Jesus has prepared a room for you in His Father's house (John 14:1–3). Your reunion with God will be one of incomprehensible joy and peace. All the sorrows of the world will be put to rest. Imagine the glory of Paul's depiction of our heavenly home:

> Behold! I tell you a mystery. We shall not all sleep, but we shall all be changed, in a moment, in the twinkling of an eye, at the last trumpet. For the trumpet will sound, and the dead will be raised imperishable, and we shall be changed. For this perishable body must put on the imperishable, and this mortal body must put on immortality. When the perishable puts on the imperishable, and the mortal puts on immortality, then shall come to pass the saying that is written:
>
> "Death is swallowed up in victory." (1 Cor. 15:51–54 ESV)

At the end of your days, you will stand face-to-face with your Creator and He will renew you in every way. This is a promise you can count on as you go through life, bringing honor and glory to Him on this side of heaven.

2

LESSONS FROM THE RABBI

Insights from the Teachings and Examples of Jesus

During Jesus's years on earth, He offered guidance for godly and effective living in daily life and offered plenty of glimpses into the world beyond this one.

Just as a friend shares insight and advice with a friend, so Jesus shared His divine wisdom with His followers. He explained what would happen to His disciples as they continued to follow Him and what kinds of treatment, trials, and tribulation they could expect to encounter on earth. He also went on to convey what they could look forward to as a reward in heaven.

The principles Jesus taught during His time on earth are just as timely and applicable today as they were when He first spoke them. Not only will these passages guide you as you navigate life here on earth, but they will draw your heart closer to the speaker Himself.

THE REWARD OF DISCIPLESHIP

Even Jesus's closest followers sometimes struggled with understanding His teachings. They had given up friends, family, and livelihoods to wander penniless with their rabbi. They would suffer persecution and death. Although they put their trust in Him, there were times when they questioned and doubted:

> Peter spoke up, "We have left everything to follow you!"
>
> "Truly I tell you," Jesus replied, "no one who has left home or brothers or sisters or mother or father or children or fields for me and the gospel will fail to receive a hundred times as much in this present age: homes, brothers, sisters, mothers, children and fields—along with persecutions—and in the age to come eternal life. But many who are first will be last, and the last first." (Mark 10:28–31)

In regard to the disciples' question as to what they would receive in eternity, Jesus replied, "No one who has left home or wife or brothers or sisters or parents or children for the sake of the kingdom of God will fail to receive many times as much in this age, and in the age to come eternal life" (Luke 18:29–30). In making these promises, Jesus was asserting that there are some rewards that are present for a believer and follower of

Christ and also other rewards that will be given abundantly in heaven. This is true for you as you seek to follow Him during your day-to-day life.

THE PROMISE OF BELIEF

When Jesus testified to Nicodemus concerning the difficulty of accepting spiritual truth, He stated,

> Just as Moses lifted up the snake in the wilderness, so the Son of Man must be lifted up, that everyone who believes may have eternal life in him. For God so loved the world that he gave his one and only Son, that whoever believes in him shall not perish but have eternal life. ...Whoever believes in the Son has eternal life, but whoever rejects the Son will not see life, for God's wrath remains on them. (John 3:14–16, 36)

In alluding to Moses's lifting up the snake in the desert, Jesus was referring to Numbers 21:6–9. When the children of Israel complained about not having food and water to their liking, God sent venomous snakes among the people and caused many to die (v. 6). When the people of Israel confessed that they had sinned, the Lord instructed Moses to make a bronze snake and place it on a pole. If the people were bitten by the snakes, they could look at the bronze snake and be healed (vv. 8–9).

Using this historical illustration, Jesus declared that He also "must be lifted up" (John 3:14). Just as in the case of the Israelites when they looked at the bronze serpent in faith and were healed, so Jesus predicted that when they looked at Him lifted up, they would believe and have eternal life (v. 15). In referring to being lifted up, Jesus was referring to His crucifixion and the need for the Israelites to go to the cross in faith in order to have salvation through Christ. Jesus concluded this with the great affirmation that the gift of God's Son was an act of love and that "whoever believes in him shall not perish but have eternal life" (v. 16). No doubt, the disciples did not understand what Jesus was referring to until after His death and resurrection.

Later, the apostle John declared, "Whoever believes in the Son has eternal life, but whoever rejects the Son will not see life, for God's wrath remains on them" (v. 36). This verse provides a marvelous prophecy that belief in Jesus as the Son assures an individual of eternal life in contrast to those who reject Him and therefore do not receive life and are under God's wrath.

NEVER THIRST AGAIN

The story of Jesus and His encounter with the woman at the well is one of the most intriguing and mystifying throughout Scripture:

> The Samaritan woman said to him, "You are a Jew and I am a Samaritan woman. How can you

ask me for a drink?" (For Jews do not associate with Samaritans.)

Jesus answered her, "If you knew the gift of God and who it is that asks you for a drink, you would have asked him and he would have given you living water."

"Sir," the woman said, "you have nothing to draw with and the well is deep. Where can you get this living water? Are you greater than our father Jacob, who gave us the well and drank from it himself, as did also his sons and his livestock?"

Jesus answered, "Everyone who drinks this water will be thirsty again, but whoever drinks the water I give them will never thirst. Indeed, the water I give them will become in them a spring of water welling up to eternal life." (John 4:9–14)

In order to better understand their interaction, it's important to know the cultural context. Jesus was journeying from Judea to Galilee, which required traveling directly through Samaria or going around by the east through Perea. Jesus and His disciples chose the direct route, which was an intentional and significant choice.

After traveling all day, Jesus and His disciples came as far as Jacob's well, which was located in Samaria, and the disciples went into the village to buy food. As Jesus sat by the well, a Samaritan woman came to draw water. Jesus, fully aware of her spiritual need, asked her for a drink (v. 7). The Samaritan woman, well aware of the antagonism between Samaritans and Jews, was surprised that He would have anything to do with her. When she questioned why Jesus was willing to ask for the drink, He said, "If you knew the gift of God and who it is that asks you for a drink, you would have asked him and he would have given you living water" (v. 10). The Samaritan woman replied, of course, that Jesus had nothing with which to draw water, and, after all, His forefathers—Jacob and his sons—had drawn water from the well. Naturally, it raised the question as to how He could give her Living Water (vv. 11–12).

Jesus then pointed out that worship is not a matter of place but rather a matter of true worship in spirit and in truth (v. 23). The Samaritan woman replied, "'I know that Messiah' (called Christ) 'is coming. When he comes, he will explain everything to us'" (v. 25). Jesus then declared to her, "I, the one speaking to you—I am he" (v. 26).

At this point in the story, the disciples had returned and were surprised that Jesus would talk to a Samaritan woman but, nevertheless, did not ask Him why. When they urged Him to eat, He replied, "I have food to eat that you know nothing about" (v. 32). When the disciples could not understand this, He told them, "My food … is to do the will of him who sent me and to finish his work" (v. 34). Jesus then pointed out to them that the fields were ripe unto harvest, speaking, of course, of a spiritual harvest.

When the woman testified to the people in her village that Jesus had told her all she had ever done, they naturally came out of curiosity to see the One who knew all about her, and many believed (vv. 39–41). The gospel of John, designed to lead people to faith in Christ that they may receive eternal life, has now added the Samaritan woman as a possible candidate for salvation along with Nicodemus, a law-abiding Jew. In the process of leading the Samaritan woman to faith in Him, Jesus had demonstrated His omniscience and His capacity to give eternal life. This promise, which Jesus made to an outcast more than two thousand years ago, extends to you in the present age.

YOU CANNOT BE SNATCHED OUT OF HIS HAND

> The Jews who were there gathered around him, saying, "How long will you keep us in suspense? If you are the Messiah, tell us plainly."
>
> Jesus answered, "I did tell you, but you do not believe. The works I do in my Father's name testify about me, but you do not believe because you are not my sheep. My sheep listen to my voice; I know them, and they follow me. I give them eternal life, and they shall never perish; no one will snatch them out of my hand." (John 10:24–28)

The sayings of Jesus divided His audience: some claimed that He was demon possessed, but others claimed that His miracles demonstrated He was a genuine prophet (vv. 19–21).

The Jews pressed Him for an explanation about His identity: "How long will you keep us in suspense? If you are the Messiah, tell us plainly" (v. 24). Jesus replied that He had given them adequate proof. His miracles testified to His claim to be genuine (v. 25). The reason they were having trouble believing Him was that they were not His sheep (v. 26). Jesus declared, "My sheep listen to my voice; I know them, and they follow me. I give them eternal life, and they shall never perish" (vv. 27–28). This passage is another assertion that those who are once born again have received an eternal salvation in the eternal life that they receive. Jesus promised that they will never perish or fall from their exalted position. He said, "No one will snatch them out of my hand. My Father, who has given them to me, is greater than all; no one can snatch them out of my Father's hand. I and the Father are one" (vv. 28–30).

As a double assurance of the certainty of their salvation, Jesus declared that they are in not only His hands but also the Father's hands and that no one can take them out of the Father's hands. When He concluded with the statement "I and the Father are one" (v. 30), the Jews recognized this as a claim to deity and picked up stones to stone Him (v. 31). Jesus asked them why they were offended. They replied, "We are not stoning you for any good work ... but for blasphemy, because you, a mere man, claim to be God" (v. 33).

Even after conversing with Jesus face-to-face, these people did not recognize His holiness. Although you have yet to stand in His presence, you will be able to follow wherever He leads because you have tuned your ear to hear His voice.

BELIEVERS HAVE VICTORY OVER DEATH

"Lord," Martha said to Jesus, "if you had been here, my brother would not have died. But I know that even now God will give you whatever you ask."

Jesus said to her, "Your brother will rise again."

Martha answered, "I know he will rise again in the resurrection at the last day."

Jesus said to her, "I am the resurrection and the life. The one who believes in me will live, even though they die; and whoever lives by believing in me will never die. Do you believe this?"

"Yes, Lord," she replied, "I believe that you are the Messiah, the Son of God, who is to come into the world." (John 11:21–27)

Because John 11 deals with the death and resurrection of Lazarus, it serves as a good introduction to the death and resurrection of Christ, which occurred not many days later. It centers on the great truth that in Jesus we have the assurance of resurrection and life.

When Jesus heard of Lazarus's illness, He declared, "This sickness will not end in death. No, it is for God's glory so that God's Son may be glorified through it" (v. 4).

For His own reasons, Jesus intentionally delayed His return so that Lazarus had been dead several days before He got there. Martha, who went out to greet Him, said, as no doubt they had said many times in His absence, "Lord … if you had been here, my brother would not have died. But I know that even now God will give you whatever you ask" (vv. 21–22). Though she did not expect Jesus to raise Lazarus, she did assert that He had the power to do it.

This gave Jesus occasion to discuss resurrection with her, and Jesus said to her, "Your brother will rise again" (v. 23). In her reply, Martha asserted her faith that all would be resurrected eventually. Jesus went on to affirm more than the hope of all for resurrection and said to her, "I am the resurrection and the life. The one who believes in me will live, even though they die; and whoever lives by believing in me will never die. Do you believe this?" (vv. 25–26). Martha in reply came back to the basic fact that she believed that Jesus was the Christ, the Son of God (v. 27).

When Jesus arrived at Lazarus's tomb, He performed perhaps His most impressive miracle. Jesus prayed to God the Father, "Father, I thank you that you have heard me. I knew that you always hear me, but I said this for the benefit of the people standing here, that they may believe that you sent me" (vv. 41–42).

Then Jesus, speaking with a loud voice, said, "Lazarus, come out!" (v. 43). To the astonishment of those who observed, Lazarus came out of the tomb with his grave clothes. Jesus ordered the people to take the grave clothes from him and let him go (v. 44).

The obvious great miracle that occurred influenced many others to put their trust in Jesus (v. 45), but the chief priests and the Pharisees were upset by this demonstration of the power of

God and said, "Here is this man performing many signs. If we let him go on like this, everyone will believe in him, and then the Romans will come and take away both our temple and our nation" (vv. 47–48).

Even in the face of miraculous events, the Pharisees remained blind to the significance of what had happened at the tomb of Lazarus. If your eyes have been opened to the truth about Jesus Christ, you can be assured that these promises are meant for you and that, like Lazarus, you will triumph over death.

HE WILL BRING YOU HOME

"Do not let your hearts be troubled. You believe in God; believe also in me. My Father's house has many rooms; if that were not so, would I have told you that I am going there to prepare a place for you? And if I go and prepare a place for you, I will come back and take you to be with me that you also may be where I am. You know the way to the place where I am going."

Thomas said to him, "Lord, we don't know where you are going, so how can we know the way?"

Jesus answered, "I am the way and the truth and the life. No one comes to the Father except through me. If you really know me, you will know my Father as well. From now on, you do know him and have seen him." (John 14:1–7)

The disciples were deeply troubled. They had heard Jesus announce that one was going to betray Him. They had heard Him tell Peter that he was going to deny Him three times. Most of all, they were concerned about the fact that Jesus had said He was going to leave them and they could not follow Him (13:36). At this point of their last night together, Jesus prophetically outlined God's provisions for them as troubled disciples in a troubled world.

Jesus, first of all, exhorted the disciples not to be troubled. He said, "Believe in God; believe also in me" (14:1). This command can be literally translated, "Keep on trusting in God; keep on trusting in me." The secret of having an untroubled heart in a troubled world is to trust God completely. In exhorting them to do this, He was giving the whole answer. However, because all of us, including the disciples, are weak, the rest of the chapter outlines the support basis for this trust in God.

In the light of His departure, Jesus promised them that He would return: "My Father's house has many rooms; if that were not so, would I have told you that I am going there to prepare a place for you? And if I go and prepare a place for you, I will come back and take you to be with me that you also may be where I am" (vv. 2–3).

This was an entirely new revelation to be contrasted to Christ's earlier revelation concerning His second coming to judge the world. This was a coming with an entirely different context, and its purpose was to take the disciples out of the world and to the Father's house, which clearly refers to heaven, where Jesus has gone before to prepare a place for those who believe in Him.

This is the first reference in the New Testament to what Paul later referred to as the rapture of the church (1 Cor. 15:51–58; 1 Thess. 4:13–18).

The disciples were both emotionally and theologically unprepared to receive this truth, which John recorded many years later in this gospel. They did comprehend, however, that Jesus was going to leave them. This was devastating to them because they had been with Christ for three and a half years and had left their homes and occupations to be His disciples. They simply did not understand what Jesus meant when He said He was going to leave them. Scripture records that Jesus had closed His remarks by saying, "You know the way to the place where I am going" (John 14:4).

Thomas, as he contemplated what Jesus was saying, did not know where Jesus was going, and probably the other disciples had the same problem. Thomas said to Jesus, "Lord, we don't know where you are going, so how can we know the way?" (v. 5). This was a logical statement because if one does not know his destination, he does not know where he is going. This is a profound truth that affects all of our lives. Knowing our ultimate destination is a part of God's program of reassuring troubled disciples. On the other hand, Jesus was referring to heaven, and certainly Thomas and the other disciples should have known that this was their ultimate destination.

Jesus's answer to Thomas was both profound and simple: "I am the way and the truth and the life. No one comes to the Father except through me" (v. 6). There are few statements in any language or book that can rival this for profound truth.

Jesus is the way—the road—to heaven. This is not accepted by the world but is the mainstay of Christians who put their trust in God.

Jesus also is the truth. All things are true because of God's laws and revelation, and Jesus is the source of this order in the universe. All truth is true only as it is related in some way to Jesus Christ as the truth.

Jesus declared, "I am ... the life" (v. 6). Again, this is the profound truth that only belief in Jesus provides eternal life and blessing in the life to come. All the philosophies of the world and the schemes of men have never been able to substitute anything for God's plan of Jesus as the way to heaven as the ultimate test of truth and the ultimate bestower of eternal life.

In addition to the great truth that Christ Himself was going to indwell believers, a dispensational truth characteristic of the present age from Pentecost was predicted in verse 20: "On that day you will realize that I am in my Father, and you are in me, and I am in you." The expression "I am in you" refers to Christ indwelling, but "you are in me" presents a truth foreign to the Old Testament but realized by Christians baptized into Christ. The gracious provision of God is not only that God is in us but also that we are vitally related to Jesus Christ and share the same eternal life. It is not too much to say that verse 20 is one of the great revelations of the New Testament and characterizes the present age as a distinct dispensation.

Once again, Jesus referred to the need to obey His commands and love Him. He promised, "The one who loves me will be loved by my Father, and I too will love them and show myself to them" (v. 21). The disciples did not show much interest in the fact of the love of Christ or being loved by the Father, but Judas (not Iscariot) asked the question: "But, Lord, why do you intend to show yourself to us and not to the world?" (v. 22). Jesus replied that a new relationship existed between Jesus and the disciples as well as the Father and the disciples. Jesus said, "Anyone who loves me will obey my teaching. My Father will love them, and we will come to them and make our home with them" (v. 23). Not only Jesus and the Holy Spirit would indwell a believer; God the Father would also make his body His home. Those who do not love Jesus and obey Him know nothing of this marvelous truth (v. 24).

The final work of God on behalf of the troubled disciples was His marvelous peace: "Peace I leave with you; my peace I give you. I do not give to you as the world gives. Do not let your hearts be troubled and do not be afraid" (v. 27). This remarkable statement came from Jesus, who knew that in the next twenty-four hours He would die the awful death of crucifixion and His body would be in the tomb. What did Jesus mean by "my peace"? The peace that Christ was referring to goes beyond the prophecy of death and resurrection of Christ and beyond ascension to the ultimate disposal and judgment of all things.

Jesus knew that in the end God would triumph and His death on the cross would be rewarded by the heritage of millions of souls being saved. He also knew that, though the disciples were troubled, their troubles were temporary and their ultimate peace was to be realized.

The peace that Jesus gives is more than psychological peace, more than an act of human will, and one of the marvelous things that comes when a disciple of Jesus who puts his faith in God realizes the tremendous assets and provisions the Father has made for him as a Christian. Because of this, it is possible to be at peace even while living in a troubled world.

INHERITING GLORY

True believers in Christ are coheirs with Him, meaning that they will inherit all the blessings of the Father. During the time that we live on earth, we are given the Holy Spirit, who shapes us into the likeness of Jesus Christ. Even though this does not produce a perfect moral life, it nevertheless characterizes the believer who is living under the new nature rather than the old. Present experience of salvation is the forerunner of that which is prophesied. If the believer is now a child of God, then he is also the heir of God. As such, we may share some sufferings in this present life, but we also will share in the glory to come. The apostle Paul wrote,

> I consider that our present sufferings are not worth comparing with the glory that will be revealed in us. For the creation waits in eager expectation for the children of God to be revealed. For the creation was subjected to frustration, not by its own choice, but by the will of the

one who subjected it, in hope that the creation itself will be liberated from its bondage to decay and brought into the freedom and glory of the children of God.

We know that the whole creation has been groaning as in the pains of childbirth right up to the present time. Not only so, but we ourselves, who have the firstfruits of the Spirit, groan inwardly as we wait eagerly for our adoption to sonship, the redemption of our bodies. For in this hope we were saved. (Rom. 8:18–24)

Contrasting our present suffering with future glory helps us realize what Paul stated: "I consider that our present sufferings are not worth comparing with the glory that will be revealed in us" (v. 18). The suffering of a Christian is paralleled by suffering in the world as a whole, for all creation is groaning and hurting like a woman giving birth (vv. 22–23). When a Christian suffers, he all the more anticipates the full meaning of being adopted as a son of God. Though this takes place in our present lives, when God recognizes a Christian as His son, it gives a basis for hope that ultimately the sufferings will cease and makes it possible to hope patiently (v. 25). Even though a Christian may not know how to pray under some circumstances, the promise is given that the Holy Spirit will pray as his intercessor (vv. 26–27).

Because we have been saved, we enter into the divine process of ultimate glorification described by Paul:

> Those God foreknew he also predestined to be
> conformed to the image of his Son, that he might
> be the firstborn among many brothers and sisters.
> And those he predestined, he also called; those he
> called, he also justified; those he justified, he also
> glorified. (vv. 29–30)

All of this is based on grace, as we have been chosen and our salvation is possible because God did not spare His own Son (v. 32). There is no danger of a Christian ever coming into condemnation and being declared lost. This is because he is seen in Christ, who died and was resurrected and is supported by His present intercession in heaven: "Christ Jesus who died—more than that, who was raised to life—is at the right hand of God and is also interceding for us" (v. 34).

The complete safety of the believer is presented in the classic conclusion of Romans 8, in which Paul declared that nothing can separate a Christian from the love of Christ:

> I am convinced that neither death nor life, nei
> ther angels nor demons, neither the present nor
> the future, nor any powers, neither height nor
> depth, nor anything else in all creation, will be
> able to separate us from the love of God that is in
> Christ Jesus our Lord. (vv. 38–39)

Although it is true that a Christian may face death and suffering as a martyr, it is also true that a Christian conquers through Christ, who loves him. We have certain hope that what God has promised will certainly be fulfilled.

3

RAPTURE READY

You Could Be Taken Out of the World

The moment we put our hope in Jesus Christ, we began a journey unlike any other. From that moment forward, our lives have been spent straddling two worlds. This life, with its constant concerns, demands our immediate attention, yet we know that there are unseen battles being waged all around us and we play a key role in them. We are eternal creatures living in a temporal realm.

Jesus's disciples fully understood this dichotomy. When they asked Jesus for specific information about His return, He replied, "About that day or hour no one knows, not even the angels in heaven, nor the Son, but only the Father" (Matt. 24:36). Perhaps anticipating that His followers might grow weary and waver in their commitment to His ways, Jesus impressed upon them the importance of remaining diligent: "You also must be ready, because the Son of Man will come at an hour when you do not expect him" (v. 44).

The hope of eternity with Jesus is a constant source of rejuvenation when the cares of the world wear us down. But it's easy to forget that Jesus promised to reclaim this realm and that His triumphant return could happen before you draw your next breath.

What will the rapture look like? What will happen to you and your loved ones if you are alive at the time of Jesus's glorious second coming? How should you live your day-to-day life in light of eternity? These passages will illuminate what the Bible tells us about Jesus's return and, possibly, your involvement with it.

THE DAY OF THE LORD VERSUS THE DAY OF CHRIST

> You will shine among them like stars in the sky
> as you hold firmly to the word of life. And then
> I will be able to boast on the day of Christ that I
> did not run or labor in vain. (Phil. 2:15–16)

When it comes to the topic of the rapture, it's important to have a clear understanding of the terminology. There are two expressions that are commonly used interchangeably but actually concern two different events.

First is the expression "the day of the Lord." In Scripture, the day of the Lord normally pertains to an extended period of time in which God acts in judgment of the world. This is developed, for instance, in 1 Thessalonians 5, where the apostle Paul exhorts believers to continue to live righteously so that they would "be kept blameless at the coming of our Lord Jesus Christ" (v. 23).

The day of Christ refers to the external events that we can expect to see during the rapture. Paul employed the expression "the day of Christ Jesus" throughout his letters to the church at Philippi. In Philippians 1:6, Paul explained that the good works God has assigned to us will be brought to completion on the day of Christ. Our toil in this world will be brought to a close and a new chapter will begin, both for believers and unbelievers alike.

THE RAPTURE REVEALED

> Brothers and sisters, we do not want you to be uninformed about those who sleep in death, so that you do not grieve like the rest of mankind, who have no hope....
>
> For the Lord himself will come down from heaven, with a loud command, with the voice of the archangel and with the trumpet call of God, and the dead in Christ will rise first. After that, we who are still alive and are left will be caught up together with them in the clouds to meet the Lord in the air. And so we will be with the Lord forever. (1 Thess. 4:13, 16–17)

Along with 1 Corinthians 15:51–58, this passage in Thessalonians is one of the crucial revelations regarding the rapture of the church. Though the Old Testament and the Synoptic Gospels reveal much about the second coming of Christ, the specific revelation concerning His coming to take His church out of the world, both living and dead, was not revealed until John 14:1–2, the night before His crucifixion. Because the apostles at that time did not understand the difference between the first and second comings of Christ, they could hardly be instructed in the difference between the rapture of the church and Christ's second coming to judge and rule over the earth. A careful study of this passage (1 Thess. 4:13, 16–17) will do much to set the matter in its proper biblical revelation.

Unlike passages that deal with the second coming of Christ and trace the tremendous events that shall take place in the years preceding it, the rapture of the church is always presented as the next event and, as such, one that is not dependent on immediate preceding events. The rapture of the church, defined in 1 Thessalonians 4:17 as being "caught up together with them in the clouds to meet the Lord in the air," is a wonderful truth especially designed to encourage Christians.

Paul stated that he did not want the Thessalonians to be uninformed or ignorant concerning Christians who had died. Thus, they were not to grieve for them as the world does, having no hope. In 1 Thessalonians 4, as in all scriptures, the sad lot of those who leave this world without faith in Christ is described in absolute terms of having "no hope" (v. 13). Only in Christ can one have hope of life to come in heaven.

The nature of the Thessalonians' faith in Christ that prompts them to believe that they will be ready when Christ comes is stated in verse 14: "We believe that Jesus died and rose again, and so we believe that God will bring with Jesus those who have fallen asleep in him."

If one can accept the supernatural event of Christ's dying for sin and rising from the grave, one can also believe in the future rapture of the church. This is defined as faith "that God will bring with Jesus those who have fallen asleep in him" (v. 14). At the rapture, believers are caught up to heaven. At the second coming, believers remain on earth. Accordingly, the event that Paul was describing here is quite different from the second coming of Christ as it is normally defined.

In what sense will Jesus bring with Him those who have fallen asleep? This refers to Christians who have died, and the expression of falling asleep is used to emphasize the fact that their death is temporary. When a Christian dies, his soul goes immediately to heaven (2 Cor. 5:6–8). Paul declared that Jesus would bring with Him the souls of those who have fallen asleep. The purpose is brought out for this in the verses that follow in that Jesus will cause their bodies to be raised from the dead and their souls will reenter their bodies.

The actual sequence of events was described by Paul:

> According to the Lord's word, we tell you that we who are still alive, who are left until the coming of the Lord, will certainly not precede those who have fallen asleep. For the Lord himself will come down from heaven, with a loud command, with

the voice of the archangel and with the trumpet
call of God, and the dead in Christ will rise first.
After that, we who are still alive and are left will
be caught up together with them in the clouds to
meet the Lord in the air. And so we will be with
the Lord forever. (1 Thess. 4:15–17)

One question the Thessalonians seemed to have faced is this: If
the Lord came for the living, would they have to wait before they
could see those who were resurrected from the dead? This thought
was set at rest when Paul stated, "We who are still alive, who are
left until the coming of the Lord, will certainly not precede those
who have fallen asleep" (v. 15). In verse 16, the sequence of events
is described. The Lord Jesus Himself will come down from heaven;
that is, there will be a bodily return to earth. Jesus will utter a
loud command related to the resurrection of the dead and the
translation of the living. This will be accompanied by the voice of
the archangel, which will be followed by the trumpet call of God.
When this sounds, the event will take place. Christians who have
died will rise first. Then Christians still living, being translated into
bodies suited for heaven, "will be caught up together with them in
the clouds to meet the Lord in the air" (v. 17).

For all practical purposes, these events will take place at the
same time. Those living on earth who are translated will not have
to wait for the resurrection of Christians who have died because, as
a matter of fact, they will be resurrected a moment before. In saying that those who "are left will be caught up together with them

in the clouds," Paul was expressing the essential character of the rapture, which is a snatching up or a bodily lifting up of those on earth, whether living or resurrected, their meeting the Lord in the air, and then their triumphant return to heaven. This is described as being "with the Lord forever" (v. 17).

This is in keeping with the original revelation of the rapture in John 14:1–3, where Christ informed His disciples that He was coming for them to take them to the Father's house in heaven. They will remain in heaven until the great events describing the period preceding the second coming of Christ will take place, and the church in heaven will participate in the grand procession described in Revelation 19 of His return from heaven to earth to set up His earthly kingdom.

The mention of clouds (1 Thess. 4:17) is taken by some to be literal clouds, as was true of Christ's ascension (Acts 1:9). Some believe that the great number of those raptured will resemble a cloud, similar to the reference of Hebrews 12:1. The glorious prospect is that once this takes place, there will be no more separation between Christ and His church.

The locale of their future is not permanent, as they will be in heaven during the time preceding the second coming. They will be on earth during the millennial kingdom and then will inhabit a new heaven and new earth in eternity. In each of these situations, they will be with Christ in keeping with the symbolism of their marriage to Him as the heavenly Bridegroom.

Most significant in this passage is the fact that there are no world-shaking events described as leading up to this event. As a matter of fact, the church down through the centuries expected the rapture to happen at any time, a hope that continues today. By contrast, the second coming of Christ will be preceded by divine judgments on the world and followed by the establishing of Christ's earthly kingdom. No mention is made of that here, but the emphasis is placed on the wonderful fellowship Christians will enjoy with the Savior. The wonderful hope of the rapture of the church is a source of constant encouragement to those who put their trust in Him and are looking forward to His coming.

WHEN WILL THE RAPTURE HAPPEN?

> The end of all things is near. Therefore be alert and
> of sober mind so that you may pray. (1 Pet. 4:7)

Although we can't know the precise date of the rapture, God hasn't left us in the dark about His plan. The day of the Lord is not one literal twenty-four-hour period; rather, it is a period of time during which the events of God's judgment will take place. One of the early events of this time frame is the assembly of a ten-nation kingdom, which will be formed in the final seven years leading up to the second coming. Because the day of the Lord will begin as a time period when the rapture occurs, the two events are linked as both beginning without warning and coming without a specific sign. However, as time progresses after the rapture, there will be noticeable signs that the world is in the day of the Lord and in the period leading up to the second coming, just as there will be signs that the millennial kingdom has begun after the second coming. As the rapture must precede the signs, it necessarily must occur when the day of the Lord begins.

One of the important signs of the day of the Lord is the fact that the people will be saying, "Peace and safety," when, as a matter of fact, "destruction will come on them suddenly, as labor pains on a pregnant woman, and they will not escape" (1 Thess. 5:3). This is the period between the rapture and the second coming, and according to Daniel 9:27, this period will last seven years. The first half of this period will be a time of peace when a covenant of peace will be made with Israel, as indicated in Daniel 9:27. During this period, people will hail peace as having been achieved, as mentioned in 1 Thessalonians 5:3. Then suddenly the great tribulation will begin and they will not escape its judgment. The earth-shattering judgments that precede the second coming are described graphically in Revelation 6–18.

Because Christians are forewarned that the day of the Lord is coming, they should not be surprised and should live in the light of God's divine revelation. "You, brothers and sisters, are not in darkness so that this day should surprise you like a thief. You are all children of the light and children of the day. We do not belong to the night or to the darkness" (1 Thess. 5:4–5). The day of the Lord is pictured here as a time of night for the world because it is a time of judgment, differing from the Christian's day, which is a day of light. The Christian's day will be climaxed by the rapture; the day for the wicked will begin at that time, and the judgments related to the day of the Lord will take place according to the time sequence of this period, with the great judgments occurring in the great tribulation, cresting in the second coming.

These events are often portrayed in books and movies as epic and terrifying. Indeed, the judgment of the Lord is a fearsome thing, and the rapture will be a time unlike any other in human history. But it is important to remember that you, an adopted child of God, have nothing to fear. Paul assures his readers of their fate in verse 9: "God did not appoint us to suffer wrath but to receive salvation through our Lord Jesus Christ." For this reason, every child of God can think on the rapture with hope.

Paul realized that some Christians would have died before the rapture and that others would still be living. Accordingly, he said of Christ, "He died for us so that, whether we are awake or asleep, we may live together with him" (v. 10). His reference to being awake meant Christians being still alive in the world; being asleep meant that Christians have died and their bodies will be sleeping in the grave though their souls are in heaven. His conclusion here, as in the other prophetic truths revealed in this epistle, is a practical one: "Encourage one another and build each other up, just as in fact you are doing" (v. 11).

WHO WILL BE RAPTURED?

> Do not let your hearts be troubled. You believe
> in God; believe also in me. My Father's house

has many rooms; if that were not so, would I
have told you that I am going there to prepare
a place for you? And if I go and prepare a place
for you, I will come back and take you to be
with me that you also may be where I am.
(John 14:1–3)

When they first heard that Jesus was going away, the apostles'
immediate reaction was fear and concern. With this comforting
promise, Jesus described the rapture to His closest followers to
assuage their fears.

My Father's house has many rooms; if that were
not so, would I have told you that I am going
there to prepare a place for you? And if I go and
prepare a place for you, I will come back and
take you to be with me that you also may be
where I am. (vv. 2–3)

This was a brand-new revelation in contrast to Jesus's earlier
revelation concerning His second coming to judge the world. The
arrival He announced would be an entirely different context, with
its purpose to take His followers out of the world. He would escort
them to the Father's house—a clear reference to heaven—where
Jesus had gone before to prepare a place for those who believe in
Him. These verses make up the first instance in the New Testament
to what Paul later referred to as the rapture of the church.

THE FATE OF BELIEVERS PAST AND PRESENT

> We will not all sleep, but we will all be changed—
> in a flash, in the twinkling of an eye, at the last
> trumpet. For the trumpet will sound, the dead
> will be raised imperishable, and we will be
> changed. For the perishable must clothe itself
> with the imperishable, and the mortal with
> immortality. When the perishable has been
> clothed with the imperishable, and the mortal
> with immortality, then the saying that is written
> will come true: "Death has been swallowed up in
> victory." (1 Cor. 15:51–54)

This is perhaps one of the most incredible and astounding prophecies concerning the rapture. Not only will living Christians be caught up to heaven without dying, but those Christians who have died will also be resurrected. Both will receive new bodies suited for heaven. As Paul stated, the bodies will be imperishable and never subject to decay, as well as immortal (1 Cor. 15:53). They will also be free from sin and be the objects of God's grace and blessing throughout eternity.

At the rapture of the church, there will be a victory over death and the grave. Paul stated, "Death has been swallowed up in victory. 'Where, O death, is your victory? Where, O death, is your sting?'" (vv. 54–55). Paul was quoting from Isaiah 25:8,

which states that God "will swallow up death forever," and from
Hosea 13:14, where God stated,

> I will deliver this people from the power of the
>   grave;
>   I will redeem them from death.
> Where, O death, are your plagues?
>   Where, O grave, is your destruction?

This doctrine is stated with greater clarity in the New
Testament, where Paul traced the victory through Jesus Christ:
"Thanks be to God! He gives us the victory through our Lord Jesus
Christ" (1 Cor. 15:57).

In light of the great doctrine of the resurrection and translation and the imminent hope of the Lord's return, believers are
exhorted to make the most of their remaining time on earth. Paul
stated, "My dear brothers and sisters, stand firm. Let nothing
move you. Always give yourselves fully to the work of the Lord,
because you know that your labor in the Lord is not in vain"
(v. 58). Believers should stand firm because they are planted on
the rock Christ Jesus and on the sure promises of God. They
should not allow the instabilities and hardships of life to sway
them from confidence in God. While living out their lives on
earth, they are to engage in the work of the Lord always as to
time and fully as to extent because they know that after this
life at the judgment seat of Christ, they will be rewarded. This
great passage dealing with the rapture of the church coupled

with Paul's earlier revelation (1 Thess. 4:14–17) constitute the principal passages on the Lord's coming and the bright hope that it could be soon.

REJECTING TEMPORARY GLORY IN EXCHANGE FOR ETERNAL REWARD

> The grace of God has appeared that offers salvation to all people. It teaches us to say "No" to ungodliness and worldly passions, and to live self-controlled, upright and godly lives in this present age, while we wait for the blessed hope— the appearing of the glory of our great God and Savior, Jesus Christ, who gave himself for us to redeem us from all wickedness and to purify for himself a people that are his very own, eager to do what is good. (Titus 2:11–14)

It's no secret that this world is full of temptations both great and seemingly trivial. It's easy to become distracted by the pursuit of earthly fulfillment. Career success, relational harmony, reputation, and respect are just a few of the distractions we face on a daily basis. Knowing how difficult it can be to keep our eyes on the prize, Paul stated that the gospel of salvation "teaches us to say 'No' to ungodliness and worldly passions, and to live self-controlled, upright and godly lives in this present age" (v. 12).

The fuel that keeps us moving in the right direction is hope. As we live our lives, we cling to the most incredible promise. As Paul expressed it, "While we wait for the blessed hope—the appearing of the glory of our great God and Savior, Jesus Christ" (v. 13). This hope is related to the rapture of the church rather than to the second coming of Christ to set up His kingdom, but the question has been raised as to why it is described as a "glorious appearing." At His second coming, Jesus will appear in a glorious event described in Revelation 19:11–16, an event that all the world will see (1:7). Conversely, the rapture of the church is never described as visible to the world.

The question, therefore, remains: How can the rapture be described as a glorious event—as an event that reveals the glory of God? The answer is quite simple. The world will not see the glory of Christ at the time of the rapture as at the time of the second coming, but Christians will behold Him in His glory, and to them it will be a magnificent appearing. As stated in 1 John 3:2, "What we will be has not yet been made known. But we know that when Christ appears, we shall be like him, for we shall see him as he is."

Christians will be changed into bodies that are sinless in order to behold the Lord in His holy splendor. The fact that we will "see him as he is" (that is, His glorious person) is evidence that the Christians will have been transformed, which will make it possible for them to see Him in His glory. The expectation of seeing Christ as He is in glory is another reason to turn away from the temporal triumphs of this world and instead live hon-orable lives.

CLING TO THE PROMISE

> You need to persevere so that when you have done the will of God, you will receive what he has promised. For,

> "In just a little while,
>   he who is coming will come
>   and will not delay." (Heb. 10:36–37)

When troubles surround you on all sides, it's tempting to fall into despair. We all wonder, from time to time, if there's anything better on the horizon. As the Christian looks forward to relief from the present persecutions and difficulties, the promise is given, "He who is coming will come and will not delay." The reference, no doubt, is to the rapture of the church when every Christian, whether living or dead, will be caught up with the Lord. This will end the conflicts of this life and usher in the peace we can expect to have when we sit in His presence.

The fact that life will not go on forever should be an encour-agement to Christians who are going through deep trouble. A Christian's pilgrimage on earth is temporary and soon may be cut short by the rapture of the church. This should serve as a stimulus to faithful service and endurance even when persecutions and trials may be the lot of an individual Christian.

As these last few prophecies have shown us, the rapture is not meant to scare or worry us or cause us to lose sleep. Instead, the rapture is a hope and a finish line. We may suffer in this present world of brokenness and sin, but our Lord will not abandon us. He is coming back to take us away from all this, and we will truly experience the great joy that the word *rapture* originally intended.

4

JOY TO THE WORLD

Believers Will Enjoy a Thousand Years of Peace on Earth

From the moment He drew His first breath, Jesus has brought joy to those who put their hope in Him. As the disciple and gospel writer Luke recalled in the story of Jesus's birth, "The angel said to them, 'Do not be afraid. I bring you good news that will cause great joy for all the people'" (Luke 2:10). This joy still burns in the hearts of believers two thousand years after His ascension into heaven. It is this joy that compels us to live pure and God-pleasing lives as we await Jesus's return.

Just as our ancestors passed away without seeing Jesus's return, so we may also do the same. But Scripture instructs us to live as though He could arrive at any moment. With that in mind, it's prudent to seek to understand what might happen upon His return. How long will Jesus reign, and what will that look like? What will Satan's role be during this time? What about the roles of families, nations, and the earth itself? These are important questions, and a careful study of Scripture will bring us closer to a solid understanding.

A THOUSAND YEARS AND MANY QUESTIONS

> I saw thrones on which were seated those who had been given authority to judge. And I saw the souls of those who had been beheaded because of their testimony about Jesus and because of the word of God. They had not worshiped the beast or its image and had not received its mark on their foreheads or their hands. They came to life and reigned with Christ a thousand years.... This is the first resurrection. Blessed and holy are those who share in the first resurrection. The second death has no power over them, but they will be priests of God and of Christ and will reign with him for a thousand years. (Rev. 20:4–6)

One major question has been asked by believers for centuries: Will there be a thousand-year reign of Christ before or after His second coming? There are many schools of thought, but for our purposes, we'll discuss the premillennial, postmillennial, and amillennial views.

First, the simplest way to describe pre- and postmillennial thought is to say that each holds that the fulfillment of the millennium is achieved before His second coming, with amillenarians more or less explaining away any literal fulfillment.

The majority view of premillenarians is that the kingdom following the second coming of Christ is a fulfillment of God's theocratic program and is in keeping with the promise given to David that his kingdom and throne would continue forever over Israel. Those who interpret the prophecies literally view Christ as reigning supremely over the entire world as a political leader, beginning with the second coming. This viewpoint is often called the dispensational point of view, but a better description would be that they hold to a literal kingdom on earth. Basically, this view takes into consideration the fact that Christ fulfills in a literal way what was prophesied in the Scripture concerning the kingdom on earth.

The amillennial interpretation, which is probably the majority view of the church today, tends to minimize the promise of a kingdom on earth. Amillenarians do not all agree as to how to arrive at this conclusion. Their viewpoint is called amillennial because their view is that there will be no literal kingdom on earth with Christ reigning on the throne.

Some feel, as Augustine, that the entire present age is the millennial kingdom and that God is reigning in the hearts of those who put their trust in Him. This, of course, does not provide any literal fulfillment of the millennial kingdom.

Some hold that the millennial kingdom is being fulfilled in heaven through Christ's spiritual reign over the earth. Often they do not consider the period a literal thousand years, and they minimize the literal meaning of the prophecies relating to it.

Some amillenarians now hold that the millennium will be fulfilled in a new heaven and new earth in eternity and, therefore, does not need to be fulfilled now. The problem with all of these points of view is that they do not provide adequate explanations of many passages in the Old Testament and New Testament that teach a literal kingdom. This is true also of Revelation 20.

MAJOR MOMENTS DURING THE MILLENNIUM

> He will not judge by what he sees with his eyes,
>   or decide by what he hears with his ears;
> but with righteousness he will judge the needy,
>   with justice he will give decisions for the
>   poor of the earth.
> He will strike the earth with the rod of his
>   mouth;
>   with the breath of his lips he will slay the
>   wicked.
> Righteousness will be his belt
>   and faithfulness the sash around his waist.
>   (Isa. 11:3–5)

The millennial kingdom, which will run its course before the events that climax it, is described at length in many passages in Scripture. Though the exact figure of one thousand years is not mentioned except in Revelation 20, the fact of a kingdom that has long duration is clearly the intent of the prophetic passages (Isa. 2:2–4; 11:4–9; Ps. 72). According to the Old Testament, Jerusalem will be the capital of the millennial kingdom (Isa. 2:2–3). War will cease (v. 4). The millennial kingdom will be characterized by righteousness, and there will be justice for all the oppressed (11:3–5). Even the ferocity of beasts will be tamed (vv. 6–9). Isaiah summarized the thought in verse 9:

> They will neither harm nor destroy
>   on all my holy mountain,
> for the earth will be full of the knowledge of the
>   LORD
>   as the waters cover the sea.

Psalm 72, as well as many other psalms, gives the glowing prophetic picture of the future millennium. The future is described as flourishing and the government as righteous, and abundant peace is promised as long as the moon endures. All kings bow down before Christ, and His rule extends from sea to sea. The earth will be filled with the glory of God. The desire of nations for peace, righteousness, knowledge of the Lord, economic justice, and deliverance from Satan will have its prophetic fulfillment. The major factors of the millennium, including Christ's absolute power, will include perfect and righteous government and ideal circumstances on earth. In many respects, the rule of Christ as the last Adam replaces what God had intended for Adam, who was placed in charge of the garden of Eden.

Many passages in the Old Testament emphasize the fact that Israel will have a prominent place. According to Ezekiel 20:33–38, at the time of the second coming, Israel will experience a purging judgment and only the righteous, godly remnant will be allowed to enter the kingdom. Israel, pictured in the Old Testament as being an untrue wife, will now be rejoined to Christ in the symbol of marriage and experience His love (Hos. 1:10–11; 2:14–23).

Though Israel will enjoy the blessings of being regathered to her ancient land and under the special rule of Christ, the rest of the world will also experience the rule of Christ as King of Kings. The nation of Israel, however, will also have the benefits of the rule of David, resurrected from the dead as a regent of Christ.

THE DAWN OF THE MILLENNIAL KINGDOM

> The LORD will be king over the whole earth. On
> that day there will be one LORD, and his name the
> only name. (Zech. 14:9)

The millennial kingdom will be distinguished by the fact that the Lord, Jesus Christ as the Messiah of Israel and King of Kings, will rule over the entire earth (v. 9). Included in the topographical changes will be the elevation of Jerusalem as described in verse 10. From that day forward, Jerusalem will be secure and will never be destroyed again.

An indication of the rule of Christ as King of Kings and Lord of Lords is that He will judge the nations that fought against Jerusalem (vv. 12–13). A plague will seize man and beast alike, but a great quantity of gold, silver, and clothing will accrue to Israel's benefit (vv. 14–15).

Those who survive the judgments at the beginning of the millennial kingdom will be required to worship Christ annually (v. 16). If they do not worship Him as commanded, God will hold their rain (vv. 17–19). It will be a time when the holiness of God is especially revealed and false elements like the Canaanites will be shut out (vv. 20–21). The partial revelation of the nature of the millennial kingdom as described here is amplified in many other passages in both the Old and New Testaments.

A KINGDOM FORGED BY GLORY

In that day the Branch of the LORD will be beautiful and glorious, and the fruit of the land will be the pride and glory of the survivors in Israel. Those who are left in Zion, who remain in Jerusalem, will be called holy, all who are recorded among the living in Jerusalem. The Lord will wash away the filth of the women of Zion; he will cleanse the bloodstains from

> Jerusalem by a spirit of judgment and a spirit
> of fire. Then the LORD will create over all of
> Mount Zion and over those who assemble there
> a cloud of smoke by day and a glow of flaming
> fire by night; over everything the glory will be a
> canopy. It will be a shelter and shade from the
> heat of the day, and a refuge and hiding place
> from the storm and rain. (Isa. 4:2–6)

The expression "in that day" sometimes refers to the contemporary scene and sometimes to the future millennium, as determined by the context. In this passage, the beauty of the millennial reign is described.

Isaiah predicted cleansing of the bloodstains of Jerusalem and the presence of the Lord over Mount Zion, signified by a cloud of smoke by day and fire by night (v. 5). In the millennial kingdom, the day will come when Israel will be cleansed from sin and her glory restored (Zeph. 3:14–20).

A PEACEFUL PICTURE OF THE MILLENNIUM

> A little while, and the wicked will be no more;
>   though you look for them, they will not be
>   found.
> But the meek will inherit the land
>   and enjoy peace and prosperity.

> The wicked plot against the righteous
>   and gnash their teeth at them;
> but the Lord laughs at the wicked,
>   for he knows their day is coming.
>   (Ps. 37:10–13)

David declared his delight in the Lord and expressed his confidence that as one commits his way to the Lord, he will receive what his heart desires. He spoke also of the future revelation of the righteousness and justice of his cause. David predicted judgment on the wicked and that the meek would inherit the land. He predicted also that the wicked would perish and the Lord would uphold the righteous. David expressed his faith that the Lord would protect His own and give them the land for an inheritance (vv. 27–29).

THE CAPITAL OF THE KINGDOM

> In the last days
>
>   the mountain of the LORD's temple will be
>   established
>   as the highest of the mountains;
>   it will be exalted above the hills,
>   and all nations will stream to it.
>
> Many peoples will come and say,

> "Come, let us go up to the mountain of
> the LORD,
> to the temple of the God of Jacob.
> He will teach us his ways,
> so that we may walk in his paths."
> (Isa. 2:2–3)

The prophet Isaiah predicted the future kingdom of the Messiah. Jerusalem is described as the capital of the world in a time of peace rather than war, a time when the Lord Himself will teach and instruct the people in His ways.

THE COMING SON OF DAVID

> Nevertheless, there will be no more gloom for
> those who were in distress....
>
> The people walking in darkness
> have seen a great light;
> on those living in the land of deep darkness
> a light has dawned.
> You have enlarged the nation
> and increased their joy;
> they rejoice before you
> as people rejoice at the harvest,
> as warriors rejoice
> when dividing the plunder. (Isa. 9:1–3)

The coming of the Messiah was compared to when a great light would shine and be a time of joy and rejoicing. The period was thought to be a victorious one for Israel.

The great prophecy of the coming of Christ is recorded in verses 6–7:

> To us a child is born,
>> to us a son is given,
>> and the government will be on his
>>> shoulders.
> And he will be called
>> Wonderful Counselor, Mighty God,
>> Everlasting Father, Prince of Peace.
> Of the greatness of his government and peace
>> there will be no end.
> He will reign on David's throne
>> and over his kingdom,
> establishing and upholding it
>> with justice and righteousness
>> from that time on and forever.
> The zeal of the LORD Almighty
>> will accomplish this.

This passage is one of the most important messianic prophecies of the Old Testament describing Christ as possessing the attributes of God. He will be "Everlasting Father" (v. 6), not in the sense of being God the Father, the first person of the Trinity, but in the sense that He will be like a father in His government over Israel in the millennial kingdom. The peace of that period was indicated in the title "Prince of Peace."

As God promised David, his kingdom would go on forever, being fulfilled by the millennial kingdom. God will continue to be sovereign over creation throughout eternity to come. The prophecy specified that His throne would be David's throne (v. 7), in fulfillment of the Davidic covenant indicating that this throne, like David's kingdom, would be on earth, not in heaven. The kingdom will be realized by the power of God: "The zeal of the LORD Almighty will accomplish this" (v. 7).

These prophecies, as interpreted in their literal sense, predict fulfillment of the expectation of a kingdom on earth after the second coming of Christ, in keeping with the premillennial interpretation of Scripture. In this passage, as in many passages in the Old Testament, the first and second coming of Christ are not distinguished, and the child who was born (v. 6) in Bethlehem in His first coming will be the same person described as the Everlasting King who will reign forever (v. 7).

FROM DESOLATE TO DAZZLING

> For Zion's sake I will not keep silent,
> 　　for Jerusalem's sake I will not remain quiet,
> till her vindication shines out like the dawn,
> 　　her salvation like a blazing torch.
> The nations will see your vindication,

and all kings your glory;
   you will be called by a new name
      that the mouth of the LORD will bestow.
You will be a crown of splendor in the
      LORD's hand,
   a royal diadem in the hand of your God.
      (Isa. 62:1–3)

Another beautiful prophetic picture of the future kingdom is revealed as following the second coming of Christ. At that time, Jerusalem's salvation will be evident to all. The nations surrounding Israel will observe her righteousness and glory. Israel is compared to a crown, or a royal diadem. Though she once was described as desolate, now she will be called Hephzibah, meaning "my delight is in her," and her land Beulah, meaning "married one," for "the LORD will take delight in you, and your land will be married" (v. 4). Her restoration is described as a joyful marriage.

Israel will never have to surrender to foreigners her new wine or her crops. Israel was challenged to prepare the road for the King. The people of Israel will be described as "the Holy People."

A KINGDOM OF PEACE AND JOY

Be glad and rejoice forever
   in what I will create,
for I will create Jerusalem to be a delight
   and its people a joy.

I will rejoice over Jerusalem
>   and take delight in my people;
the sound of weeping and of crying
>   will be heard in it no more.

Never again will there be in it
>   an infant who lives but a few days,
>   or an old man who does not live out his
>   years;
the one who dies at a hundred
>   will be thought a mere child. (Isa. 65:18–20)

A glorious picture was presented of an ultimate new heaven and new earth. The prophet then returned to the theme of Jerusalem in the millennial kingdom, in which there will be longevity but also death. One who dies at one hundred years will be considered still a youth. The millennial earth will provide Israel with security: "They will build houses and dwell in them; they will plant vineyards and eat their fruit" (v. 21). By contrast, the wicked will not take possessions away from the people of Israel: "My chosen ones will long enjoy the work of their hands" (v. 22). Israel's children will not be "doomed to misfortune" (v. 23). Tranquility in nature will also occur:

The wolf and the lamb will feed together,
>   and the lion will eat straw like the ox,
>   and dust will be the serpent's food.

> They will neither harm nor destroy
>   on all my holy mountain. (v. 25)

These prophecies do not fit the eternal New Jerusalem but relate to the millennium.

In expressing Israel's future hope, the Old Testament often mingled prophecies of the millennial kingdom with the foretelling of the New Jerusalem in eternity. The distinctions are made clear when the details are observed. Here, evidently, the millennial kingdom was being described, because in the New Jerusalem there will be no death, no sin, and no judgment. The millennial kingdom will be a time of great joy and rejoicing and deliverance for the people of God, but death and sin will still be present.

CHRIST'S POWER IN THE MILLENNIAL KINGDOM

> In my vision at night I looked, and there before me was one like a son of man, coming with the clouds of heaven. He approached the Ancient of Days and was led into his presence. He was given authority, glory and sovereign power; all nations and peoples of every language worshiped him. His dominion is an everlasting dominion that will not pass away, and his kingdom is one that will never be destroyed. (Dan. 7:13–14)

The coming of the Son of Man could be understood to refer to the coming of Jesus Christ as the Messiah in His second coming, as Christ Himself used the expression "the Son of Man" in many references to Himself in the book of Matthew (8:20; 9:6; 10:23; 11:19; 12:8, 32, 40).

This passage mentions Jesus Christ in His incarnation approaching "the Ancient of Days" (Dan. 7:13), an obvious reference to God the Father. The reference to giving Him complete authority over all peoples will be fulfilled in His millennial kingdom, which, as far as dominion is concerned, will continue forever (v. 14).

THE TEMPLE ESTABLISHED

In the last days

> the mountain of the LORD's temple will be
>   established
>   as the highest of the mountains;
> it will be exalted above the hills,
>   and peoples will stream to it.

Many nations will come and say,

> "Come, let us go up to the mountain of the
>   LORD,
>   to the temple of the God of Jacob.

He will teach us his ways,
                    so that we may walk in his paths."
                        (Mic. 4:1–2)

In this passage, Micah described the glorious future kingdom. The first three verses of chapter 4 are almost identical to
Isaiah 2:2–4. The glorious temple will be established "in the last
days" (Mic. 4:1). This has its fulfillment in the millennium when
Ezekiel's temple (Ezek. 40–44) will be built. As far as Micah's
foresight was concerned, the temple could have been established
soon, as he did not contemplate the intervention of the present
age of the church. People from all over the world will come to
visit the Lord's temple.

Even the Gentiles will seek to come to the temple. They will
say, "He will teach us his ways, so that we may walk in his paths"
(Mic. 4:2). Zion and Jerusalem will be the center from which the
Law goes forth. The contemporary situation in the kingdom will
be one of peace because "they will beat their swords into plow-
shares and their spears into pruning hooks. Nation will not take up
sword against nation, nor will they train for war anymore" (v. 3).
The people will be at peace and "everyone will sit under their own
vine and under their own fig tree, and no one will make them
afraid, for the LORD Almighty has spoken" (v. 4). In this kingdom
period, the Lord will rule them in Mount Zion and restore the
governmental dominion of Zion. These prophecies will be fulfilled
in the millennial kingdom.

> The remnant of Jacob will be
>> in the midst of many peoples
> like dew from the LORD,
>> like showers on the grass,
> which do not wait for anyone
>> or depend on man.
> The remnant of Jacob will be among the
>> nations,
>> in the midst of many peoples,
> like a lion among the beasts of the forest,
>> like a young lion among flocks of sheep,
> which mauls and mangles as it goes,
>> and no one can rescue.
> Your hand will be lifted up in triumph over your
>> enemies,
>> and all your foes will be destroyed.
>> (5:7–9)

Though Assyria invaded Israel's land and conquered her for a time, ultimately the people of Israel will prevail and be like a lion among the beasts of the forests. Micah predicted that all their foes would be destroyed. When that day comes, God will bring about the destruction of that which is evil in the midst of Israel: their chariots (v. 10), their witchcraft, their carved images (vv. 12–13), and the Asherah poles (v. 14). God's vengeance will be against Israel as well as the nations (v. 15).

THE VERY LAST REBELLION

> When the thousand years are over, Satan will
> be released from his prison and will go out to
> deceive the nations in the four corners of the
> earth—Gog and Magog—and to gather them for
> battle. In number they are like the sand on the
> seashore. They marched across the breadth of the
> earth and surrounded the camp of God's people,
> the city he loves. But fire came down from heaven
> and devoured them. And the devil, who deceived
> them, was thrown into the lake of burning sulfur,
> where the beast and the false prophet had been
> thrown. They will be tormented day and night
> for ever and ever. (Rev. 20:7–10)

John described the climax of the millennial kingdom as one
last battle against Satan. Satan and his attackers come from all
nations of the world. They gather about the city of Jerusalem in
attempting to capture the capital city, but fire comes down from
heaven and devours them. There will be no earthly aftermath to
this battle at the end of the millennium. Life does not go on after
this battle, for the world immediately moves into a new heaven
and new earth situation.

While the pursuit of understanding is important to a rever-
ent believer, the important thing to keep in mind is that faithful

believers will be invited to spend eternity in God's everlasting kingdom. Though the details of these prophecies are fascinating and merit careful study, they should never take the place of trusting in God's character. There are certainly details about the end times that we cannot fathom. When we encounter gray areas, we can take comfort in knowing that He is mighty and just and will be faithful to save.

5

RECKONING AND RECOMPENSE

Judgment Day with a Gracious God

There's no topic shrouded in more mystery and intrigue than the end times. Countless books, movies, and television shows have portrayed this subject, yet most people feel a sense of uncertainty about it. Questions about judgment day abound: What will come of mankind? What will happen to the earth and everything in it? What will happen in the heavens when these incredible events are set in motion?

For most people, the questions surrounding judgment day are even more personal: What can I expect to happen to me? Will judgment be the frightening experience we often envision it to be?

God, the Author and Perfecter of life, has not overlooked any detail. He has considered and planned every moment of that important day. Scripture is full of specific prophecies regarding Christ's judgment of all creation—including you, His dearly beloved child.

WAITING ON SALVATION

> Just as people are destined to die once, and after that to face judgment, so Christ was sacrificed once to take away the sins of many; and he will appear a second time, not to bear sin, but to bring salvation to those who are waiting for him. (Heb. 9:27–28)

For children of God, His grace is made manifest everywhere. We see evidence of His mercy and love all around us. Still, a Christian living in this present age of grace is reminded that it is part of God's righteous government that every individual will be judged.

The coming judgment for all people makes most clear the necessity of entering by faith into the grace of God, which is provided through the death of Christ. Though judgment is certain, those who have entered into grace at the present age will find that their judgment is a gracious one. You, as a believer in Christ, can look forward to an evaluation of your life and service as a basis for reward.

CREATION IS SWEPT AWAY

> "I will sweep away everything
>   from the face of the earth,"
>   declares the LORD.
> "I will sweep away both man and beast;
>   I will sweep away the birds in the sky

and the fish in the sea—
and the idols that cause the wicked to
stumble."

"When I destroy all mankind
on the face of the earth,"
declares the LORD. (Zeph. 1:2–3)

Speaking specifically of the ultimate judgment of God on the entire earth at the time of the second coming of Christ, Zephaniah declared the word of the Lord. This message depicts God's power in perfect clarity. We often think of God as Creator, and rightfully so. Everything in this world was crafted by His hand. Yet Scripture also tells us that He gives and takes away (Job 1:21). Although we are right to be awestruck by His creative powers, we would be remiss to forget that God reserves the right to destroy as He sees fit.

At the appropriate time, everything on earth—from plants and animals to the tallest mountains—will be swept away from the face of the earth. Clearly, the wicked will remain on earth without the beauty of God's creation to enjoy and sustain them.

JESUS WILL SENTENCE AND PARDON

The Father loves the Son and shows him all he does. Yes, and he will show him even greater works than these, so that you will be amazed. For just as the Father raises the dead and gives them life, even so the Son gives life to whom he is pleased to give it. Moreover, the Father judges no one, but has entrusted all judgment to the Son, that all may honor the Son just as they honor the Father. Whoever does not honor the Son does not honor the Father, who sent him.

Very truly I tell you, whoever hears my word and believes him who sent me has eternal life and will not be judged but has crossed over from death to life. (John 5:20–24)

Jesus's life was one of perfect righteousness. He spent His time on earth being wrongly persecuted. He suffered unjustly all the way to the cross, where he took the punishment for our sins. Scripture is filled with examples of Jesus modeling this kind humility.

Because Jesus had healed the invalid at the pool of Bethesda on the Sabbath, the Jews persecuted Him (John 5:2–16). Because He claimed God as His Father, the Jews persecuted Him all the more because they regarded this as a statement that He was equal to the Father (vv. 17–18).

Jesus declared that His oppression wouldn't last forever. Describing His union with the Father, Jesus explained that the Father loves Him (v. 20), that the Son has the power to raise the dead even as the Father does (v. 21), and that the Father has entrusted all judgment to the Son (vv. 22–23). Accordingly, he who does not honor the Son does not honor the Father (v. 23).

This led Jesus to say, "Very truly I tell you, whoever hears my word and believes him who sent me has eternal life and will not be judged but has crossed over from death to life" (v. 24).

Expanding further on His ability to save, Jesus said,

> Very truly I tell you, a time is coming and has now come when the dead will hear the voice of the Son of God and those who hear will live. For as the Father has life in himself, so he has granted the Son also to have life in himself. And he has given him authority to judge because he is the Son of Man.
>
> Do not be amazed at this, for a time is coming when all who are in their graves will hear his voice and come out—those who have done what is good will rise to live, and those who have done what is evil will rise to be condemned. (vv. 25–29)

The broad prophecies revealed by the Savior here predict, first of all, the salvation of individuals who hear the facts about Christ and as a result of believing will live eternally. Just as Jesus has life in Himself from the Father, so He has authority to judge as the Son of Man (vv. 26–27). For further confirmation of Christ's ability, Jesus called attention to the fact that those in the grave, referring to those who have died physically, will someday hear His voice and come out of the grave with the result that they will be judged concerning their lives on earth, whether good or bad (vv. 28–29).

In these predictions and assertions, the apostle John recorded one fact after another supporting his belief that Jesus is the Son of God, who has been given the keys to life as well as the ability to sentence those who deny His lordship. You, as a saved child of God and coheir with Christ, can look forward to Jesus's eternal pardon.

STANDING IN HIS PRESENCE

> For this very reason, Christ died and returned to life so that he might be the Lord of both the dead and the living.
>
> You, then, why do you judge your brother or sister? Or why do you treat them with contempt? For we will all stand before God's judgment seat. It is written:
>
> "'As surely as I live,' says the Lord,
> 'every knee will bow before me;
>   every tongue will acknowledge God.'"
>
> So then, each of us will give an account of ourselves to God. (Rom. 14:9–12)

The subject of Romans 14 is how gray areas in the Christian life should be handled. This section of Scripture is useful today as we wait on the Lord. Here, Paul addresses the question of whether Christians should eat meat that had been previously offered to idols. The Christian community was divided on this matter. Some said that meat is meat regardless of what happened to it before they bought it; others claimed that, by buying it, they participated in the worship of idols it involved.

The lesson emerging from the situation is that we should not judge our Christian brethren, especially in areas where there is difference of opinion as to the right thing to do. As Paul pointed out, the important fact is that Christ died and was resurrected so that He might be Lord over both the dead and the living: "For this very reason, Christ died and returned to life so that he might be the Lord of both the dead and the living" (v. 9). In view of this, Paul declared that Christians should not judge each other, especially in the area of evaluating the ministry of a brother. "You, then, why do you judge your brother or sister? Or why do you treat them with contempt? For we will all stand before God's judgment seat" (v. 10).

Paul gave further exposition of the judgment seat of Christ elsewhere, such as,

> No one can lay any foundation other than the one already laid, which is Jesus Christ. If anyone builds on this foundation using gold, silver, costly stones, wood, hay or straw, their work will be shown for what it is, because the Day will bring it to light. It will be revealed

with fire, and the fire will test the quality of each person's work. If what has been built survives, the builder will receive a reward. If it is burned up, the builder will suffer loss but yet will be saved—even though only as one escaping through the flames. (1 Cor. 3:11–15)

Do you not know that in a race all the runners run, but only one gets the prize? Run in such a way as to get the prize. Everyone who competes in the games goes into strict training. They do it to get a crown that will not last, but we do it to get a crown that will last forever. Therefore I do not run like someone running aimlessly; I do not fight like a boxer beating the air. No, I strike a blow to my body and make it my slave so that after I have preached to others, I myself will not be disqualified for the prize. (9:24–27)

We must all appear before the judgment seat of Christ, so that each of us may receive what is due us for the things done while in the body, whether good or bad. (2 Cor. 5:10)

The matter of judgment, or evaluation, of a brother's ministry is committed to Christ alone. Inasmuch as all Christians will stand before the judgment seat of Christ to be evaluated, believers should concentrate on their own problems instead of on the problems of others.

The absolute certainty of this judgment is stated in a recap of Isaiah 45:23: "'As surely as I live,' says the Lord, 'every knee will bow before me; every tongue will acknowledge God'" (Rom. 14:11). Scripture is clear in both the Old and New Testaments that every individual will stand before God's judgment, not necessarily at the same time or for the same reason. The assessment at the judgment seat of Christ is for those who have been saved, who will then be evaluated as to their contribution to the Lord's work.

Paul continued to summarize this: "Each of us will give an account of ourselves to God" (v. 12). This resembles the responsibility of a steward, or trustee, who has responsibility for handling the business affairs of another and eventually reporting what he does with it. In life, Christians are endowed with spiritual and natural gifts that differ. No two Christians are exactly alike, and no two Christians have exactly the same opportunities, but each will be required to give an account for what he has done with them. Undoubtedly, the more a person has, the greater his responsibility.

The issue here is not success but rather the question of faithfulness in using what God has given to an individual Christian. This is the main goal of an individual Christian's life, but we should be mindful to refrain from judging our fellow Christians. Instead, we should be preoccupied with the fact that our own lives will be judged by the most important audience: the Lord Himself.

FACING THE FINAL CONSEQUENCE OF SIN

> There will be trouble and distress for every human being who does evil: first for the Jew, then for the Gentile; but glory, honor and peace for everyone who does good: first for the Jew, then for the Gentile. For God does not show favoritism.
>
> All who sin apart from the law will also perish apart from the law, and all who sin under the law will be judged by the law. For it is not those who hear the law who are righteous in God's sight, but it is those who obey the law who will be declared righteous. (Rom. 2:9–13)

Sin not only affects us here on earth by preventing us from enjoying intimacy with God; it also has a grave eternal implication. Paul explained what would become of those who never repented of their sin, saying,

> Because of your stubbornness and your unrepentant heart, you are storing up wrath against yourself for the day of God's wrath, when his righteous judgment will be revealed. God "will repay each person according to what they have done." To those who by persistence in doing good seek glory, honor and immortality, he will give

eternal life. But for those who are self-seeking and
who reject the truth and follow evil, there will be
wrath and anger. (vv. 5–8)

Earlier in Romans 2, Paul argued that all fall short of God's
moral standards and, therefore, should not pass judgment on
others. He summarized, "When you, a mere human being, pass
judgment on them and yet do the same things, do you think you
will escape God's judgment?" (v. 3). Because all have sinned, as
Paul made clear later (3:23), salvation is by faith and by grace.

There is, however, a different quality of life in those who are
saved from those who are not saved. Those who persist in being
unrepentant, as Paul stated, face certain judgment from God. In
speaking of "the day of God's wrath" (2:5), Paul was not referring to
any specific day. Scripture unfolds the series of judgments that will
characterize the judgment of all men, and the final judgment will
come at the end of the millennial kingdom (Rev. 20:11–15). Those
who are saved have a different quality of life that demonstrates
they have come to God in repentance and faith. Accordingly, their
manner of life will be rewarded and result in eternal life. The life
of doing good and receiving eternal life is unmistakenly not possible unless a person believes and accepts the truth of God's gospel
(Rom. 2:6–8).

Though Paul was dealing primarily with Gentiles, he made
it clear that Jews are in the same situation: "There will be trouble
and distress for every human being who does evil: first for the Jew,
then for the Gentile; but glory, honor and peace for everyone who

does good: first for the Jew, then for the Gentile. For God does
not show favoritism" (vv. 9–11). The difference between Jew and
Gentile is that the Jew has been given the revelation of the Law
and the Gentile has not, but this does not change the fundamental
requirements of doing what is right in God's sight.

In verses 12–13, Paul specifically addressed the distinction
between those who sin while knowing the Law and those who do
not. Paul used the word *law* in a number of different senses in his
epistles. The point he made is that those who are under the Mosaic
Law who are Jews will be judged by it but that the Gentiles have
a general moral law and, if they are living in the will of God, will,
to some extent, conform to the Mosaic Law in its moral teachings.
Paul stated,

> (Indeed, when Gentiles, who do not have the law,
> do by nature things required by the law, they are
> a law for themselves, even though they do not
> have the law. They show that the requirements
> of the law are written on their hearts, their con-
> sciences also bearing witness, and their thoughts
> sometimes accusing them and at other times even
> defending them.) This will take place on the day
> when God judges people's secrets through Jesus
> Christ, as my gospel declares. (vv. 14–16)

Because all men have a conscience that distinguishes right
from wrong, and because God deals with the hearts of men, even

if they are not Jews under the Mosaic Law, they will be judged on the moral code they recognize as witnessed by their conscience.

In dealing with the day of judgment, Paul had in mind that God will judge Christians at the time of the rapture, as brought out in his writing in 1 Corinthians 3:11–15 and 9:24–27. The unsaved, however, will not be judged finally until after the millennial kingdom. In life, however, God also deals judgment to those who rebel against Him, and they experience His wrath, as expressed in history.

True children of God do not need to fear this kind of judgment from Him. Instead, judgment takes on a whole new meaning for those who ally themselves with Christ.

YOUR NAME WRITTEN IN HIS HANDWRITING

> Just as people are destined to die once, and after that to face judgment, so Christ was sacrificed once to take away the sins of many; and he will appear a second time, not to bear sin, but to bring salvation to those who are waiting for him. (Heb. 9:27–28)

In the mysterious chapters of Revelation 20–21, we partake in a holy vision given to the apostle John, who witnessed the final days of the world. In this vision, we see the fearsome power of God sitting side by side with His beautiful, gentle grace.

As John watched, he saw this great judgment taking place:

> I saw the dead, great and small, standing before the throne, and books were opened. Another book was opened, which is the book of life. The dead were judged according to what they had done as recorded in the books. The sea gave up the dead that were in it, and death and Hades gave up the dead that were in them, and each person was judged according to what they had done. Then death and Hades were thrown into the lake of fire. The lake of fire is the second death. Anyone whose name was not found written in the book of life was thrown into the lake of fire. (Rev. 20:12–15)

As this text makes plain, this is the final judgment. As the righteous have already been judged, this judgment relates to the wicked. This is the final resurrection, not the first resurrection, which had to do with the righteous (John 5:29; Acts 24:15).

The fact that both small and great are specified is similar to descriptions previously used in Revelation (11:18; 13:16; 19:5, 18). Those standing before the throne come from all walks of life but now are being judged on the basis of their works. According to Hebrews 9:27, everyone has to face Christ in judgment. The judgment is based on what occurs in the books that record their works and whether their names are in the Book of Life.

The Book of Life includes the names of all who are genuinely saved. If you have submitted yourself to the lordship of Christ, you can rest assured that your name will be found there, next to the names of believers past and present.

6

RECEIVE YOUR FULL REWARD

Good Things Come to Those Who Faithfully Serve

In the previous chapters, we've seen how God uses Scripture to communicate His future plans for those who love Him. These prophecies bring tremendous hope for those who wait on Him. It's hard to imagine the splendor of our eternal reward. Paul summed up the feeling of anticipation and wonder, saying,

As it is written:

"What no eye has seen,
    what no ear has heard,
and what no human mind has conceived"—
    the things God has prepared for those
        who love him. (1 Cor. 2:9)

Surely, the full reward of a life spent in fellowship with and obedience to Christ is beyond our human comprehension. Still, God gives us a peek into what we can look forward to when we spend eternity in His presence.

HIS EXALTATION BRINGS US HEALING

> "Just as Moses lifted up the snake in the wilderness, so the Son of Man must be lifted up, that everyone who believes may have eternal life in him."
>
> For God so loved the world that he gave his one and only Son, that whoever believes in him shall not perish but have eternal life. (John 3:14–16)

In alluding to Moses's lifting up the snake in the desert, Jesus was referring to Numbers 21:6–9. When the children of Israel complained about not having food and water to their liking, God sent venomous snakes among the people and caused many to die (v. 6). When the people of Israel confessed that they had sinned, the Lord instructed Moses to make a bronze snake and place it on a pole, and if the people were bitten by the snakes, they could look at the bronze snake and be healed (vv. 8–9).

Using this historical illustration, Jesus declared that He also "must be lifted up" (John 3:14). Just as in the case of when the Israelites looked at the bronze serpent in faith and were healed, so Jesus predicted that when people looked at Him lifted up, they would believe and have eternal life (v. 15). When He referred to being lifted up, Jesus was pointing to His crucifixion and the need for people to go to the cross in faith in order to have salvation through Christ. Jesus concluded this with the great affirmation that the gift of God's Son was an act of love and that "whoever believes in him shall not perish but have eternal life" (v. 16). No doubt, the disciples did not understand what Jesus was referring to until after His death and resurrection.

At the end of John 3, the writer declared, "Whoever believes in the Son has eternal life, but whoever rejects the Son will not see life, for God's wrath remains on them" (v. 36). This verse provides a marvelous prophecy that belief in Jesus as the Son assures an individual of eternal life, whereas those who reject Jesus not only do not receive life but also are under God's wrath.

A REWARD FOR A JOB WELL DONE

> Serve wholeheartedly, as if you were serving the Lord, not people, because you know that the Lord will reward each one for whatever good they do, whether they are slave or free.
>
> And masters, treat your slaves in the same way. Do not threaten them, since you know that he who is both their Master and yours is in heaven, and there is no favoritism with him. (Eph. 6:7–9)

Christians are exhorted to serve the Lord even as slaves serve their masters. If anything, Christians should do better. Christians are assured that the Lord will reward them for what has been done in their service for God, and this is regardless of whether one is a slave or free.

Bearing in mind the ultimate reward of the church in heaven, earthly masters are urged to treat their earthly slaves in a kind way (v. 9). The Ephesians passage serves as a good reminder to us in the here and now as we strive to serve our friends, family, employers, and employees in a manner that is above reproach. At the end of our mortal lives, we will reap the rewards of a job well done.

OUR NEW, GLORIFIED BODIES

> Our citizenship is in heaven. And we eagerly await a Savior from there, the Lord Jesus Christ, who, by the power that enables him to bring everything under his control, will transform our lowly bodies so that they will be like his glorious body. (Phil. 3:20–21)

In today's heated political discourse, the topic of citizenship is contentiously debated. The most common questions that arise in this conversation are: "Who is qualified to be a citizen of a country?" and "What should a government expect of its citizens, and what should citizens expect from their government?" Legislators have used countless bills and measures to try to shed light on these tricky questions. But there's more to citizenship than what can be defined on paper.

Belonging to a particular nation means that you have been endowed with a heritage and you participate in aspects of the culture. The same is true of your heavenly citizenship, which is where your true identity is rooted. By writing your name in the Book of Life, God Himself has taken care of the "on paper" details of your citizenship in heaven. What will become of your identity—who you are, what you look like, and how you feel—when you enter your new home?

Paul addressed these questions in his letter to the church at Philippi. Even as we fulfill our callings here on earth, we are citizens of heaven, governed by the unseen power of God at work in our lives.

The same power that enables a Christian to bring his life under control will also ultimately transform the body he has in this life to a body "like his glorious body" (v. 21).

Paul is referring here to the fact that a believer's resurrection body will be patterned after the resurrection body of Christ. This body will be of flesh and bone but without sin, decay, or death. In speaking of the believer's body as glorious, it does not mean that it will emanate brilliant light, as is sometimes true of God Himself, as in the transfiguration of Christ, and as revealed of God in heaven. The glory of which he is speaking here is in reference to the fact that the glory of God is the manifestation of His infinite perfections. Though the believer may not have a body that glows with light in a similar way as the transfigured body of Christ (Matt. 17:1–2), his body will nevertheless reflect God's perfections.

Your resurrection body will be holy as God is holy, immortal as God is immortal, everlasting as God is everlasting. It will be a constant reminder of the extent of God's grace, which took those who were justifiably destined for eternal punishment and transformed them into saints whose resurrection, or translation, introduced them to lives wholly committed to God.

ADORNED WITH THE CROWN OF LIFE

> Consider it pure joy, my brothers and sisters, whenever you face trials of many kinds, because you know that the testing of your faith produces perseverance....
>
> Blessed is the one who perseveres under trial because, having stood the test, that person will receive the crown of life that the Lord has promised to those who love him. (James 1:2–3, 12)

Those who will trust in the Lord in a time of trial are especially blessed. Believers will be rewarded in heaven for their faithfulness to the Lord. Often these rewards are characterized as crowns:

- Everyone who competes in the games goes into strict training. They do it to get a crown that will not last, but we do it to get a crown that will last forever. (1 Cor. 9:25)

- My brothers and sisters, you whom I love and long for, my joy and crown, stand firm in the Lord in this way, dear friends! (Phil. 4:1)
- What is our hope, our joy, or the crown in which we will glory in the presence of our Lord Jesus when he comes? Is it not you? (1 Thess. 2:19)

Persecutions may bring humiliation and suffering on earth, but when they are endured, they will bring a beautiful reward in heaven. This is a tremendous comfort to those who have faced trials of every kind. The fact that we have eternal life will be a crown that will set us apart as belonging to the Lord.

RECEIVING AN INHERITANCE

Praise be to the God and Father of our Lord Jesus Christ! In his great mercy he has given us new birth into a living hope through the resurrection of Jesus Christ from the dead, and into an inheritance that can never perish, spoil or fade. This inheritance is kept in heaven for you, who through faith are shielded by God's power until the coming of the salvation that is ready to be revealed in the last time. (1 Pet. 1:3–5)

Just as good parents feel joy at the prospect of leaving a good inheritance for their children, so God delights in giving an unending reward to His children. In keeping with the "living hope" given Christians "through the resurrection of Jesus Christ" (v. 3), we have a future inheritance that is being kept for us: "and into an inheritance that can never perish, spoil or fade … kept in heaven for you" (v. 4).

Meanwhile, as we wait for our inheritance, God protects us: "through faith [we] are shielded by God's power until the coming of the salvation that is ready to be revealed in the last time" (v. 5). This inheritance is certain because of God's promise in grace. Peter goes on to say that persecutions and trials in Christ demonstrate the genuineness of a believer's faith.

A WARM WELCOME INTO GOD'S KINGDOM

> Make every effort to confirm your calling and election. For if you do these things, you will never stumble, and you will receive a rich welcome into the eternal kingdom of our Lord and Savior Jesus Christ. (2 Pet. 1:10–11)

The world may not always welcome us and our Christian testimonies, and there may be opposition even unto death, but it is still true that we can anticipate being received and publicly acknowledged as part of God's kingdom. In making sure that our faith in Christ is real, we are assured through Peter's words that we "will receive a rich welcome into the eternal kingdom."

ROOM AT CHRIST'S THRONE

> Those whom I love I rebuke and discipline. So be earnest and repent. Here I am! I stand at the door and knock. If anyone hears my voice and opens the door, I will come in and eat with that person, and they with me.
>
> To the one who is victorious, I will give the right to sit with me on my throne, just as I was victorious and sat down with my Father on his throne. (Rev. 3:19–21)

Though the book of Revelation deals primarily with prophecy, it was written to help the churches of the present age understand the purposes of God and the great events that will characterize the end of the age. In the same way, we can garner wisdom, discernment, and comfort from the prophecies contained within it.

At the conclusion of the seven messages to the churches, a general invitation was given to those who will listen and come to Christ. First of all, Christ stated the general principle: "Those whom I love I rebuke and discipline. So be earnest and repent" (v. 19). As is illustrated in the messages to the churches, Christ stated that His purpose was not to judge but to bring those whom He loves to repentance. The important fact is that His rebuke and discipline stem from His love for them. The word *discipline* has in it the thought of child training taken from childhood to adulthood. The exhortation to self-judgment and repentance is another reminder that Christians who do not judge themselves will be judged, as stated by Paul in 1 Corinthians 11:31–32: "If we were more discerning with regard to ourselves, we would not come under such judgment. Nevertheless, when we are judged in this way by the Lord, we are being disciplined so that we will not be finally condemned with the world." Because the believer has established an eternal relationship with God as one who is saved, it is revealed that God will not allow him to continue in sin indefinitely but, sooner or later, either in time or eternity, will deal with him.

Having urged them to have fellowship with Him, Christ describes Himself as waiting for them to come: "Here I am! I stand at the door and knock. If anyone hears my voice and opens the door, I will come in and eat with that person, and they with me" (Rev. 3:20). This passage has sometimes been construed to refer to salvation, but in the context, it seems to refer to those who already are believers. The issue is not related to salvation by eating with Christ but to fellowship, nourishment, and spiritual growth. God does not force Himself on anyone but waits for believers to come in simple faith to receive from God that which only God can supply.

The concept of knocking and entering is found in Scripture, of which Luke 12:35–40 is an illustration. However, in this and many other instances, the thought is that Christ is on the outside and the others who are on the inside waiting for Him to come should open the door when He comes. Christ used this in a parable: "Be dressed ready for service and keep your lamps burning, like servants waiting for their master to return from a wedding banquet, so that when he comes and knocks they can immediately open the door for him" (vv. 35–36).

The invitation Christ extends here for those who wish to come and eat with Him is most gracious and illustrates that fellowship with God is always available to those willing to put their trust in Christ and come to God. In that fellowship, they will enjoy not only the presence of the Savior but also the nourishment and strengthening that come from partaking of spiritual truth. They can be strengthened by dining on the things of God, the things of salvation, our wonderful hope, God's sustaining grace, and all the other blessings that are ours in Christ.

As Christ expresses it, "To the one who is victorious, I will give the right to sit with me on my throne, just as I was victorious and sat down with my Father on his throne" (Rev. 3:21). Those who walk with Christ in fellowship in this life will also enjoy the right of fellowship and sharing in the throne of Christ in eternity to come. This invitation is extended to any in the churches who are faithful and honor and serve the Lord. It is another illustration of the gracious provision God has made for those who trust Him.

The message to the churches closes with the same invitation repeated in the message of each church: "Whoever has ears, let them hear what the Spirit says to the churches" (v. 22). God has spoken in words that should not be misunderstood, but so much depends on individuals hearing and responding to what they hear. The tragedy is that, in so many cases, no one is listening.

Taken as a whole, the messages to the seven churches epitomize the major spiritual problems of the church down through the ages.

Ephesus represented the danger of forsaking the love that characterized believers when they first trusted Christ (Rev. 2:4). Smyrna illustrated the danger of fear, though otherwise the people were faithful to God (v. 10). The church at Pergamum was a reminder of the constant danger of doctrinal compromise (vv. 14–15). The church at Thyatira illustrated moral compromise (v. 20). The church at Sardis illustrated the danger of spiritual deadness (3:1–2). The church at Philadelphia, though faithful, was warned to hold fast to the things they believed (v. 11). Laodicea illustrated the danger of lukewarmness (vv. 15–16)—of outer religion without inner zeal and reality.

Most believers have contemplated how wonderful it would have been to sit at the feet of Jesus and hear His teachings in person. These illustrations serve as reminders from God Himself of the pitfalls we must be careful to avoid as well as the virtues we must cling to. In this way, these prophecies can be used to instruct us in how to live to the glory of God in this day and age.

7

HOME, SWEET HOME

Eternity in a Place We Can Hardly Imagine

Many people dream of completing a marathon, only to be confronted by the painful reality as their feet hit the ground mile after mile. Perhaps these people trained diligently. Perhaps they prepared with proper nutrition and hydration. Perhaps they had every intention of running the entire 26.2 miles. But somewhere along the line, exhaustion sets in and they drop out of the race.

There are moments when our time here on earth can feel the same. Where we once felt enthusiasm for the future, the reality of the day-to-day grind can leave us feeling fatigued. It's easy to fall into rhythms of tiredness and despair, but Scripture exhorts us to live differently. Rather than give up, we are called to "lay aside every weight, and sin which clings so closely, and let us run with endurance the race that is set before us" (Heb. 12:1 ESV). Wouldn't we all like to be able to live lives marked by endurance rather than exhaustion? The key to living such a life is fixing our eyes on Jesus, "the pioneer and perfecter of faith" (v. 2).

In this chapter, we'll fix our gaze on Jesus and gain a clear picture of the treasure He has prepared for us when we join Him in our eternal home. We can celebrate the fact that the race we run on earth will one day end and we will move on to a place we can hardly imagine from our current perspective.

EVERLASTING BODY

We know that if the earthly tent we live in is destroyed, we have a building from God, an eternal house in heaven, not built by human hands. Meanwhile we groan, longing to be clothed instead with our heavenly dwelling, because when we are clothed, we will not be found naked. For while we are in this tent, we groan and are burdened, because we do not wish to be unclothed but to be clothed instead with our heavenly dwelling, so that what is mortal may be swallowed up by life. Now the one who has fashioned us for this very purpose is God, who has given us the Spirit as a deposit, guaranteeing what is to come.

Therefore we are always confident and know that as long as we are at home in the body we are away from the Lord. For we live by faith, not

by sight. We are confident, I say, and would prefer to be away from the body and at home with
the Lord. So we make it our goal to please him,
whether we are at home in the body or away from
it. (2 Cor. 5:1–9)

In his second letter to the Corinthians, Paul unfolded the
great truth that our present earthly bodies, which are so temporary, will be replaced by bodies that will last forever. Our
present bodies have limitations and are subject to pain, illness,
and death, and Christians long to have their permanent bodies:
"Meanwhile we groan, longing to be clothed instead with our
heavenly dwelling, because when we are clothed, we will not be
found naked" (vv. 2–3). As Paul stated it, the "mortal may be
swallowed up by life" (v. 4).

In facing the question as to whether Christians can be abso-
lutely certain of their future resurrection, Paul pointed out that
God has given us His Holy Spirit to dwell within the believer,
which is our seal and assurance of future resurrection (Eph. 4:30).
As Paul stated here, "The one who has fashioned us for this very
purpose is God, who has given us the Spirit as a deposit, guaranteeing what is to come" (2 Cor. 5:5).

As Christians, there are two different states. While in their
present bodies, Christians are physically away from the Lord in
that they are not in His presence in heaven: "We are always confident and know that as long as we are at home in the body we are
away from the Lord. For we live by faith, not by sight" (vv. 6–7).

The alternative of being with the Lord is attractive. However, as Paul had written earlier to the Philippians,

> If I am to go on living in the body, this will mean fruitful labor for me. Yet what shall I choose? I do not know! I am torn between the two: I desire to depart and be with Christ, which is better by far; but it is more necessary for you that I remain in the body. Convinced of this, I know that I will remain, and I will continue with all of you for your progress and joy in the faith, so that through my being with you again your boasting in Christ Jesus will abound on account of me. (Phil. 1:22–26)

However, Paul stated that while still in this life, "we make it our goal to please him, whether we are at home in the body or away from it" (2 Cor. 5:9). This present life offers opportunities for service and reward as we await the new bodies we will receive in our heavenly home.

SUPPER AT THE FATHER'S TABLE

> "Let us rejoice and be glad
>   and give him glory!
> For the wedding of the Lamb has come,
>   and his bride has made herself ready.

> Fine linen, bright and clean,
> was given her to wear."

(Fine linen stands for the righteous acts of God's holy people.)

Then the angel said to me, "Write this: Blessed are those who are invited to the wedding supper of the Lamb!" And he added, "These are the true words of God."

At this I fell at his feet to worship him. But he said to me, "Don't do that! I am a fellow servant with you and with your brothers and sisters who hold to the testimony of Jesus. Worship God! For it is the Spirit of prophecy who bears testimony to Jesus." (Rev. 19:7–10)

There is no happier place on earth than a wedding reception. For the blissful bride and groom, the hours following their wedding are spent dancing, eating, and celebrating with their closest family and friends. The tone is one of jubilation, and it's that same spirit of merriment that colors John's vision of the wedding of the Lamb.

In order to understand this vision and how it pertains to us, it's important to understand the wedding customs during Christ's time on earth. At that point in history, there were three major aspects to a wedding ceremony and the ensuing festivities:

1. A marriage contract was consummated by parents of the bride and the bridegroom, and the parents of the bridegroom would pay a dowry to the parents of the bride. This was the legal marriage and would require a divorce to break the union.

2. The second step, which usually occurred a year later or at another suitable time, featured the bridegroom accompanied by his male friends going to the house of the bride at midnight with a torch parade through the streets. The bride would know he was coming and be ready with her maidens to join the procession and go back to the home of the bridegroom. This is illustrated in the parable of the virgins in Matthew 25:1–13.

3. The third phase of the wedding was a marriage supper that might go on for days, as illustrated in the wedding at Cana in John 2:1–12.

In view of this custom, it is significant that what is here announced is the wedding feast, or supper, and the implication is that the first two steps of the wedding have taken place. This would fit naturally into the prophetic fulfillment of this illustration in that the legal phase of the wedding is consummated on earth when an individual believer puts his trust in Christ as Savior. We have been bought by the blood of Christ and now belong to Christ in the sense of a betrothal.

The bride will be presented with fine linen, bright and clean, which represents the righteous acts of the saints. Ephesians 5:25–27 speaks of the preparation of the bride: "Husbands, love your wives, just as Christ loved the church and gave himself up for her to make her holy, cleansing her by the washing with water through the word, and to present her to himself as a radiant church, without stain or wrinkle or any other blemish, but holy and blameless."

In preparation for the marriage, the Savior died on the cross for His church and became the sacrifice for her sin. This led to the present work of sanctification. The church is being cleansed during her time on earth with the washing of water through the Word, meaning that the sanctifying truth of the Word of God is applied and in this way prepares the bride for her future role. The third and final state is at the rapture, when the bride is presented in her perfection. There is no stain or discoloration, no wrinkle, no blemish, but in every respect the bride is holy and blameless. This beautiful union is the result of the sanctifying work at the time of the rapture, when the church is made like Christ.

HEAVEN AND EARTH ARE MADE NEW

Then I saw "a new heaven and a new earth," for the first heaven and the first earth had passed away, and there was no longer any sea. I saw the Holy City, the new Jerusalem, coming down out of heaven from God, prepared as a bride beautifully dressed for her husband. And I heard a loud voice from the throne saying, "Look! God's dwelling place is now among the people, and he will dwell with them. They will be his people, and God himself will be with them and be their God. 'He will wipe every tear from their eyes. There will be no more death' or mourning or crying or pain, for the old order of things has passed away."

He who was seated on the throne said, "I am making everything new!" Then he said, "Write this down, for these words are trustworthy and true."

He said to me: "It is done. I am the Alpha and the Omega, the Beginning and the End. To the thirsty I will give water without cost from the spring of the water of life. Those who are victorious will inherit all this, and I will be their God and they will be my children. But the cowardly, the unbelieving, the vile, the murderers, the sexually immoral, those who practice magic arts, the idolaters and all liars—they will be consigned to the fiery lake of burning sulfur. This is the second death." (Rev. 21:1–8)

How will heaven and earth change following this incredible event? Where will God dwell? John answers these questions and more by describing his vision of a new heaven, new earth, and the New Jerusalem. Scriptural revelation gives very little information about a new heaven and new earth except that it is quite different from our present earth. The only major characteristic mentioned is that there will no longer be any sea, which differs from the present situation, where most of the earth is covered with water. As the narration goes on, it is apparent that the new earth is round, as there are directions of north, south, east, and west (v. 13), but there is no indication as to whether the new earth is larger or smaller than our present earth.

Instead of focusing on a new earth and a new heaven, Revelation deals with the subject of the Holy City, the New Jerusalem. The New Jerusalem is totally different from the old Jerusalem on the present earth and is created to be the center of population in the new earth.

God will take up residence in the New Jerusalem; in fact, the New Jerusalem will be His temple. John wrote, "'He will wipe every tear from their eyes. There will be no more death' or mourning or crying or pain, for the old order of things has passed away" (v. 4). It will be a time of rejoicing in the grace of God and the opportunity and privilege of worship and service for the Lord. The situation will be an entirely new order; as John recorded, "He who was seated on the throne said, 'I am making everything new!'" (v. 5).

In referring to Himself as "the Alpha and the Omega, the Beginning and the End" (v. 6), Christ was saying that He is the first and the last, as the first and last letters of the Greek alphabet are mentioned, and this is further defined as the beginning and the end. Christ is the eternal One, and the truths He is talking about are truths that will last forever.

The wonder of salvation by grace and the drinking of the spring of the water of life are part of the wonderful provision God has made for those who put their trust in Him. This refers to how abundant our new life in Christ will be. You, a beloved member of God's family, will inherit a beautiful home and enjoy all the blessings entitled to a coheir with Christ.

JERUSALEM, GOD'S HOME

> One of the seven angels who had the seven bowls full of the seven last plagues came and said to me, "Come, I will show you the bride, the wife of the Lamb." And he carried me away in the Spirit to a mountain great and high, and showed me the Holy City, Jerusalem, coming down out of heaven from God. It shone with the glory of God, and its brilliance was like that of a very precious jewel, like a jasper, clear as crystal. It had a great, high wall with twelve gates, and with twelve angels at the gates. On the gates were written the names of the twelve tribes of Israel. There were three gates on the east, three on the north, three on the south and three on the west. The wall of the city had twelve foundations, and on them were the names of the twelve apostles of the Lamb. (Rev. 21:9–14)

John's vision depicted the reality of the new earth. He gave special attention to the Holy City, Jerusalem, because this is where God will reside. What will the Holy City look like? Who will be there? What will the role of angels be? John's description is thorough and paints a beautiful picture of life in the New Jerusalem. The description helps us modern believers comprehend the beauty of the eternal situation in which we will find ourselves when we finally experience the New Jerusalem and the new earth.

John wrote, "One of the seven angels who had the seven bowls full of the seven last plagues came and said to me, 'Come, I will show you the bride, the wife of the Lamb.' And he ... showed me the Holy City, Jerusalem, coming down out of heaven from God" (vv. 9–10). This beautiful description can also be a source of confusion. How can a city be both a place and a bride?

Actually, the bride of Christ is composed of people who have accepted Christ in the present age and form the church, the body of Christ. The beauty of the Holy City is similar to the beauty of the bride. Obviously, a literal meaning cannot be that it is both a city and a bride, so one must complement the other.

John went on to describe the city, saying, "It shone with the glory of God, and its brilliance was like that of a very precious jewel, like a jasper, clear as crystal" (v. 11). Beginning with this verse, a number of precious jewels are mentioned as being characteristic of the New Jerusalem. Sometimes, however, it is difficult to ascertain exactly which jewel is in mind.

The city as a whole is like a precious jewel, "like a jasper, clear as crystal" (v. 11), according to John. In our present earth, the jasper stone is not clear but opaque, indicating that although the jewel looks like jasper, it actually could be some other jewel. The description that follows portrays Jerusalem as a gigantic jewel piece aglow with the glory of God and a beautiful setting for His grace to be made evident in the lives of those who have trusted Him.

The city as described by John is a very impressive one even by present standards. Though some have said that the city is not a literal city and merely symbolizes the church, the body of Christ, it seems best to consider it a literal city that, nevertheless, in its elements represents the church in some of its qualities. The wall of the city is described as great and high, which illustrates the fact that not everyone is qualified to enter into the blessings of the city. The number twelve is prominent in the description of the city as seen in the twelve gates, the twelve angels, the twelve tribes of Israel (v. 12), the twelve foundations, the twelve apostles (v. 14), the twelve pearls (v. 21), and the twelve crops of fruit (22:2). The city is also said to be twelve thousand stadia in length and the wall to be one hundred forty-four cubits in width (one hundred forty-four being twelve multiplied by twelve). The fact that the twelve gates have the names of the twelve tribes of Israel (21:12) makes clear that Israel will be part of the populace of this city.

John, in his description of the city, continued, "There were three gates on the east, three on the north, three on the south and three on the west. The wall of the city had twelve foundations, and on them were the names of the twelve apostles of the Lamb" (vv. 13–14). Though the names of the twelve apostles were not given, it is clear that just as the names of the Israelite tribes on the gates of the city prove that they are in the New Jerusalem, the names of the apostles on the twelve foundations prove that the church will be in the New Jerusalem. As the facts are put together, the New Jerusalem will be the home of the saints of all ages and the holy angels as well as God Himself.

The immensity of this city is brought out by John's statement about the angel measuring the city (v. 15). The twelve thousand stadia translated into modern terms amount to about fourteen hundred miles. The city as such would be far too large to place on the millennial earth, but on the new earth there will be plenty of room.

In this city, both Jew and Gentile will inhabit the city along with the saints of all other ages. Significant is the fact, however, that a Jew is not automatically recognized as belonging to the church, and the church is not automatically related to Israel. The distinctions between the racial Jew and the church composed of both Jews and Gentiles is maintained in this revelation.

In Hebrews 12:22–24, the inhabitants of the city are itemized:

> You have come to Mount Zion, to the city of the living God, the heavenly Jerusalem. You have come to thousands upon thousands of angels in joyful assembly, to the church of the firstborn, whose names are written in heaven. You have come to God, the Judge of all, to the spirits of the righteous made perfect, to Jesus the mediator of a new covenant, and to the sprinkled blood that speaks a better word than the blood of Abel.

In the New Jerusalem will be angels and the church and all others who could be called righteous regardless of their dispensational background. Also in the city will be God the Father, God the Son, and God the Holy Spirit.

John described in detail the beautiful stones relating to the wall:

> The wall was made of jasper, and the city of pure gold, as pure as glass. The foundations of the city walls were decorated with every kind of precious stone. The first foundation was jasper, the second sapphire, the third agate, the fourth emerald, the fifth onyx, the sixth ruby, the seventh chryso-lite, the eighth beryl, the ninth topaz, the tenth turquoise, the eleventh jacinth, and the twelfth amethyst. (Rev. 21:18–20)

These stones, having varied colors and glowing with the glory of God, presented an amazingly beautiful spectacle for John as he gazed on the city. Built on the jasper stone, which is the bottom layer of the foundation, was a brilliant sapphire, like a dark blue diamond in appearance. The third foundation was an agate stone from Chalcedon, modern Turkey, and it is believed to have been sky blue with stripes of other colors. The fourth foundation, the emerald, introduces the familiar bright-green color. The onyx is a red and white stone. The sixth foundation, ruby, is also identified as sardius stone. It is used with jasper in Revelation 4:3, describing the glory of God on the throne.

The seventh foundation is chrysolite, which is thought to have been a gold color and possibly different from the modern chrysolite stone, which is a pale green. The eighth foundation, the beryl, is a deep sea green. The ninth foundation, the topaz, is yellow green and transparent. The tenth foundation, turquoise, introduces another green color. The eleventh foundation, jacinth, is violet in color. The twelfth foundation, the amethyst, is commonly a purple.

In seeing these many colors with the brilliant light of the glory of God in the New Jerusalem, John saw a scene of indescribable beauty worthy of the God who had created it. If Christians can be thrilled by the use of colors and the creations of men, how much greater will be the New Jerusalem, which comes from the creative hand of God.

John also referred to the twelve gates, which "were twelve pearls, each gate made of a single pearl" (21:21). Obviously, these transcend any pearl such as we know in this life and are large stones but beautiful like a pearl. The streets to the city are declared to be of pure gold like transparent glass (v. 21). It is possible that all the materials of this city are translucent and that the glory of God will go through them and light up the city in a blaze of color.

John next itemized things he did not see: "I did not see a temple in the city, because the Lord God Almighty and the Lamb are its temple" (v. 22). There apparently will be no sun or moon needed to bring light to the earth because the glory of God will light the New Jerusalem (v. 23). There will be no night, either, because the glory of God will illuminate the city continuously

(v. 25). John stated, "The nations will walk by its light, and the kings of the earth will bring their splendor into it" (v. 24).

The nations, referring to the Gentiles, will bring their glory and honor into the city to the glory of God (v. 26). Anything that is impure, however, or shameful or deceitful is shut out of the city and not permitted to inhabit it. As John stated it, "But only those whose names are written in the Lamb's book of life" (v. 27) will be allowed in the city. Though the description of John is graphic and presents a beautiful display of the glory of God, it is obvious that the real city that believers will see in the eternal state will far exceed it.

THE ETERNAL STATE

> The angel showed me the river of the water of life, as clear as crystal, flowing from the throne of God and of the Lamb down the middle of the great street of the city. On each side of the river stood the tree of life, bearing twelve crops of fruit, yielding its fruit every month. And the leaves of the tree are for the healing of the nations. No longer will there be any curse. The throne of God and of the Lamb will be in the city, and his servants will serve him. They will see his face, and his name will be on their foreheads. There will be no more night. They will not need the light of a lamp or the light of the sun, for the Lord God will give them light. And they will reign for ever and ever. (Rev. 22:1–5)

In the final chapter of the book of Revelation, John recorded the major features of eternal life and the circumstances of the saints in eternity. Clearly, it is a time of unqualified blessing. In keeping with the holiness and perfection of the eternal state, the water of life is issued from the throne of God and of the Lamb. The water of life speaks of the purity, power, and holiness of the eternal life in the heavenly city. Significant is the fact that the water proceeds from the throne of God and the Lamb. Though the throne of Christ is different from the throne of David and the millennial throne on which He sat throughout the millennial kingdom, this indicates that Christ is still with God the Father reigning over the eternal state.

In addition to picturing the water of life, John also recorded the tree of life in the city, adding that "the leaves of the tree are for the healing of the nations" (v. 2). The question is fairly asked why healing would be necessary in a situation where there is no sickness, death, sorrow, or crime. Accordingly, rather than healing, it could be understood as that which brings health. The leaves of the tree, then, would be described as bringing enjoyment of life in the New Jerusalem. As it may not be necessary to partake of the leaves of the tree in order to enjoy the eternal state forever, it apparently provides an avenue by which enjoyment can be enhanced. The healing is also said to extend to the nations—literally, the Gentiles, or the peoples. Though frequently used to distinguish Gentiles from Israel, the word would include all races in a context such as this.

As if to answer the question of whether these verses imply imperfection in the eternal state, John stated, "No longer will there be any curse. The throne of God and of the Lamb will be in the city, and his servants will serve him" (v. 3). All that spoke of sin and its penalties is wiped away in heaven, and there is nothing left that is a reminder of sin. All are blessed, not cursed. In support of this conclusion, it is revealed that God's throne and that of the Lamb will be in the city.

The question is often raised of what Christians will do in heaven. Scripture is very simple in stating that "his servants will serve him" (v. 3). In a situation where children of God will be profoundly grateful for God's grace in bringing them to this place where they can enjoy the blessings of eternal life, the love of the saints for God will show itself in an eager desire to serve Him. Whatever the task, whether humble or important, assigned to an individual, it will bring great satisfaction to be able to do something for God, who has done so much for us.

The intimacy of the servants of God with Him is indicated in that the saints will be able to see the face of God, and His name will be on their foreheads. John wrote, "They will see his face, and his name will be on their foreheads" (v. 4). The identification with God is mentioned several times previously in the book of Revelation (2:17; 3:12; 7:3; 14:1). Seeing the face of God is something that could not have been accomplished prior to the saints' resurrection and glorification. The fact that they will be able to see the face of God demonstrates that they are perfectly holy by His grace.

Just as there will be a wonderful experience of relationship and service to God, so they will enjoy His glory: "There will be no more night. They will not need the light of a lamp or the light of the sun, for the Lord God will give them light. And they will reign for ever and ever" (22:5). Darkness will be banished in the eternal state. The New Jerusalem, made of translucent materials, will be an amazing, beautiful sight as the light streams through all the various colors, not leaving any shadows. The sun and moon will be no more because they are no longer needed, but the glory of God will be the light of the city (21:23). The saints' blessed state is that they will reign with Christ forever.

As a climax to this revelation, John recorded, "The angel said to me, 'These words are trustworthy and true. The Lord, the God who inspires the prophets, sent his angel to show his servants the things that must soon take place'" (22:6).

An amazing record of God's faithfulness and sovereignty is demonstrated in history. God has put down evil and judged Satan and men. No longer will men rebel against God, but He will be sovereign in time and eternity. No trace of sin will taint the kingdom of God, but the holiness that is His own spiritual quality will be shared with the saints. Where there once was death, now there will be resurrection life; where there once was judgment and curse, there now is removal and redemption; where there once was darkness, now there is light; where there once was ugliness, now there is beauty. Joy and contentment replace sorrow, holiness, and sin; and men, instead of serving themselves and Satan, will worship God, serve Christ, and be like Christ in spiritual quality.

The final message of the book of Revelation is an invitation to partake of the water of life freely: "The Spirit and the bride say, 'Come!' And let the one who hears say, 'Come!' Let the one who is thirsty come; and let the one who wishes take the free gift of the water of life" (v. 17).

On one hand, prophecy was written to warn the sinner of God's judgment on him in the future with its appeal to come to God for the grace that He offers. Prophecy also, in contrast, describes for the saint the blessings that will be his in eternity because he serves God in time. Readers of the book of Revelation who do not have the gift of eternal life are urged to accept the gift as God's free offer to be born again by faith in Christ and be qualified to participate in what God has planned for those who love Him.

Our heavenly home will be unmatched in beauty and peace. Although the current world is plagued by sin, death, and darkness, heaven will be a place of purity, life, and light. All the sorrows of earth will be washed away and overshadowed by the awesome glory of God. Imagine the bliss of knowing that all your sins, failures, losses, and mistakes have been completely forgotten. Think of being restored to perfect unity with your heavenly Father and with the whole body of Christ. If you have put your hope in Jesus as your Savior, you can relish these promises and prophecies with the full assurance that they will be true for you.

8

WORDS TO LIVE BY

Promises from the Ultimate Promise Keeper

Scripture is the story of God's relentless, unfailing love for and pursuit of His children. The Bible is the tool He uses to make Himself known to His people and communicate His desires and instruction for them. His Word is "alive" (Heb. 4:12), meaning that it is powerful and applicable to every season of life.

Throughout the Bible, we find promises to God's children— promises for protection, sustenance, blessings, and much more. Unlike prophecies (events that will definitely occur), promises tend to be general principles that are true and reliable but not necessarily tied to any single moment in time. Still, we can trust God to deliver on His promises, for as we read in the book of Hebrews,

> Because God wanted to make the unchanging nature of his purpose very clear to the heirs of what was promised, he confirmed it with an oath. God did this so that, by two unchangeable things in which it is impossible for God to lie, we who have fled to take hold of the hope set before us may be greatly encouraged. (6:17–18)

The apostle Peter added,

> Through these he has given us his very great and precious promises, so that through them you may participate in the divine nature, having escaped the corruption caused by evil desires. (2 Pet. 1:4)

Wherever you are in life, God's promises will serve to nourish and guide you on your journey with Christ. You will also gain a glimpse of your future, as God, through His promises, tells you what you can anticipate as you follow Him.

YOUR FATHER WILL FIGHT FOR YOU

> Moses answered the people, "Do not be afraid. Stand firm and you will see the deliverance the LORD will bring you today.... The LORD will

fight for you; you need only to be still." (Exod. 14:13–14)

GOD HEARS YOU FROM HEAVEN

If my people, who are called by my name, will humble themselves and pray and seek my face and turn from their wicked ways, then I will hear from heaven, and I will forgive their sin and will heal their land. Now my eyes will be open and my ears attentive to the prayers offered in this place. (2 Chron. 7:14–15)

YOUR FEET ARE PLANTED FIRMLY

Blessed is the one
　　who does not walk in step with the wicked
or stand in the way that sinners take
　　or sit in the company of mockers,
but whose delight is in the law of the LORD,
　　and who meditates on his law day and night.
That person is like a tree planted by streams of
　　　　water,
　　which yields its fruit in season
and whose leaf does not wither—
　　whatever they do prospers. (Ps. 1:1–3)

YOU SHALL BE FILLED WITH JOY

My heart is glad and my tongue rejoices;
    my body also will rest secure,
because you will not abandon me to the realm of
        the dead,
    nor will you let your faithful one see decay.
You make known to me the path of life;
    you will fill me with joy in your presence,
    with eternal pleasures at your right hand.
        (Ps. 16:9–11)

GOD WILL WATCH OVER YOU

The LORD will keep you from all harm—
    he will watch over your life;
the LORD will watch over your coming and going
    both now and forevermore. (Ps. 121:7–8)

REPENTANCE LEADS TO INSIGHT

How long will you who are simple love your
        simple ways?
    How long will mockers delight in mockery
    and fools hate knowledge?
Repent at my rebuke!
    Then I will pour out my thoughts to you,

I will make known to you my teachings.

(Prov. 1:22–23)

LISTEN AND RECEIVE PEACE

Whoever listens to me will live in safety

and be at ease, without fear of harm.

(Prov. 1:33)

GIVE TO GOD FIRST AND BE BLESSED

Honor the LORD with your wealth,

with the firstfruits of all your crops;

then your barns will be filled to overflowing,

and your vats will brim over with new wine.

(Prov. 3:9–10)

SEEK WISDOM, ENJOY BLESSINGS

Blessed are those who find wisdom,

those who gain understanding,

for she is more profitable than silver

and yields better returns than gold.

She is more precious than rubies;

nothing you desire can compare with her.

Long life is in her right hand;

in her left hand are riches and honor.

> Her ways are pleasant ways,
> and all her paths are peace.
> She is a tree of life to those who take hold
> of her;
> those who hold her fast will be blessed.
> (Prov. 3:13-18)

THE BENEFITS OF RIGHTEOUS LIVING

> To do what is right and just
> is more acceptable to the LORD than
> sacrifice....
> Whoever pursues righteousness and love
> finds life, prosperity and honor.
> (Prov. 21:3, 21)

GENEROSITY WILL BE REWARDED

> The generous will themselves be blessed,
> for they share their food with the poor.
> (Prov. 22:9)

WAIT ON THE LORD AND BE BLESSED

> The LORD longs to be gracious to you;
> therefore he will rise up to show you
> compassion.

> For the LORD is a God of justice.
>> Blessed are all who wait for him!
>>> (Isa. 30:18)

YOU ARE HELD IN THE FATHER'S HAND

> I took you from the ends of the earth,
>> from its farthest corners I called you.
> I said, "You are my servant";
>> I have chosen you and have not rejected you.
> So do not fear, for I am with you;
>> do not be dismayed, for I am your God.
> I will strengthen you and help you;
>> I will uphold you with my righteous
>>> right hand.

> "All who rage against you
>> will surely be ashamed and disgraced;
> those who oppose you
>> will be as nothing and perish."
>>> (Isa. 41:9–11)

THE LORD WILL ANSWER YOU

This is what the LORD says, he who made the earth, the LORD who formed it and established it—the LORD is his name: "Call to me and I will answer you and tell you great and unsearchable things you do not know." (Jer. 33:2–3)

YOU WILL BE GIVEN A NEW HEART

I will give you a new heart and put a new spirit in you; I will remove from you your heart of stone and give you a heart of flesh. And I will put my Spirit in you and move you to follow my decrees and be careful to keep my laws. (Ezek. 36:26–27)

GOD WILL PROVIDE FOR YOU

Why do you worry about clothes? See how the flowers of the field grow. They do not labor or spin. Yet I tell you that not even Solomon in all his splendor was dressed like one of these. If that is how God clothes the grass of the field, which is here today and tomorrow is thrown into the fire, will he not much more clothe you—you of little faith? So do not worry, saying, "What shall we eat?" or "What shall we drink?" or "What shall we wear?" For the pagans run after all these things, and your heavenly Father knows that you need them. But seek first his kingdom and his righteousness, and all these things will be given to you as well. Therefore do not worry about tomorrow, for tomorrow will worry about itself. (Matt. 6:28–34)

GOD WILL GIVE YOU REST

Come to me, all you who are weary and burdened, and I will give you rest. Take my yoke upon you and learn from me, for I am gentle and humble in heart, and you will find rest for your souls. (Matt. 11:28–29)

YOUR FATHER WILL BE GENEROUS WITH YOU

I say to you: Ask and it will be given to you; seek and you will find; knock and the door will be opened to you. For everyone who asks receives; the one who seeks finds; and to the one who knocks, the door will be opened.

Which of you fathers, if your son asks for a fish, will give him a snake instead? Or if he asks for an egg, will give him a scorpion? If you then, though you are evil, know how to give good gifts to your children, how much more will your Father in heaven give the Holy Spirit to those who ask him! (Luke 11:9–13)

BELIEVE AND BE SAVED

If you declare with your mouth, "Jesus is Lord," and believe in your heart that God raised him from the dead, you will be saved. For it is with your heart that you believe and are justified, and it is with your mouth that you profess your faith and are saved. As Scripture says, "Anyone who believes in him will never be put to shame." (Rom. 10:9–11)

YOU ARE EMPOWERED TO RESIST TEMPTATION

No temptation has overtaken you except what is common to mankind. And God is faithful; he will not let you be tempted beyond what you can bear. But when you are tempted, he will also provide a way out so that you can endure it. (1 Cor. 10:13)

A HARVEST AWAITS YOU

Whoever sows to please their flesh, from the flesh will reap destruction; whoever sows to please the Spirit, from the Spirit will reap eternal life. Let us not become weary in doing good, for at the proper time we will reap a harvest if we do not give up. Therefore, as we have opportunity, let us do good to all people, especially to those who belong to the family of believers. (Gal. 6:8–10)

THE REWARDS OF HONOR

"Honor your father and mother"—which is the first commandment with a promise—"so that it may go well with you and that you may enjoy long life on the earth." (Eph. 6:2–3)

PEACE SHALL BE YOURS

Do not be anxious about anything, but in every situation, by prayer and petition, with thanksgiving, present your requests to God. And the peace of God, which transcends all understanding, will guard your hearts and your minds in Christ Jesus. (Phil. 4:6–7)

HE WILL MEET YOUR NEEDS

I have received full payment and have more than enough. I am amply supplied.... And my God will meet all your needs according to the riches of his glory in Christ Jesus. (Phil. 4:18–19)

GOD WILL HONOR YOUR PERSEVERANCE

Do not throw away your confidence; it will be richly rewarded.

You need to persevere so that when you have done the will of God, you will receive what he has promised. (Heb. 10:35–36)

YOUR OBEDIENCE WILL BE BLESSED

Whoever looks intently into the perfect law that gives freedom, and continues in it—not forgetting what they have heard, but doing it—they will be blessed in what they do. (James 1:25)

YOU HAVE THE POWER TO OVERCOME

Submit yourselves, then, to God. Resist the devil, and he will flee from you. Come near to God and he will come near to you. Wash your hands, you sinners, and purify your hearts, you double-minded. Grieve, mourn and wail. Change your laughter to mourning and your joy to gloom. Humble yourselves before the Lord, and he will lift you up. (James 4:7–10)

YOU ARE FORGIVEN

If we walk in the light, as he is in the light, we have fellowship with one another, and the blood of Jesus, his Son, purifies us from all sin.

If we claim to be without sin, we deceive ourselves and the truth is not in us. If we confess our sins, he is faithful and just and will forgive us our sins and purify us from all unrighteousness. (1 John 1:7–9)

OVERCOME AND BE ACKNOWLEDGED IN HEAVEN

The one who is victorious will … be dressed in white. I will never blot out the name of that person from the book of life, but will acknowledge that name before my Father and his angels. (Rev. 3:5)

YOU WILL FEEL NO MORE SORROW

He will wipe every tear from their eyes. There will be no more death or mourning or crying or pain, for the old order of things has passed away. (Rev. 21:4)

9

NOW AND THEN

How You Live Today Affects Your Life Tomorrow

One of the themes woven throughout Scripture is this: our present-day conduct—all of our actions and attitudes—greatly influences the quality of our earthly journey ahead and the heavenly rewards we will someday receive. For each person, life *today* significantly shapes life *tomorrow*.

Believers in our modern era live in an increasingly complex and chaotic world. With so much confusion to distract us, it can be difficult to "stay the course" and act in accordance with our beliefs. Thankfully, God has poured out His wisdom into Scripture, and we can turn to it any time we need clarity. Christ doesn't just want His believers to profess to love Him; He calls us to show our love by living holy, blameless lives (Col. 1:22). In this chapter, we'll examine some of the specific ways God has called us to live as His adopted and beloved children.

FOLLOW NOAH'S EXAMPLE

About that day or hour no one knows, not even the angels in heaven, nor the Son, but only the Father. As it was in the days of Noah, so it will be at the coming of the Son of Man. For in the days before the flood, people were eating and drinking, marrying and giving in marriage, up to the day Noah entered the ark; and they knew nothing about what would happen until the flood came and took them all away. That is how it will be at the coming of the Son of Man. Two men will be in the field; one will be taken and the other left. Two women will be grinding with a hand mill; one will be taken and the other left.

Therefore keep watch, because you do not know on what day your Lord will come. (Matt. 24:36–42)

Noah was a man who knew what it means to wait on God. He took painstaking efforts to be obedient to Him during the construction of the ark. In fact, he took more than a hundred years to build it. In this time, people carried on with their normal activities, as Jesus mentioned (v. 38). When the ark was finally finished, however, the situation suddenly changed. Now it was possible for the flood to come.

As Noah's neighbors observed, they saw a very strange sight: the animals marching into the ark in pairs, in almost military precision (Gen. 7:2–3). God also announced to Noah, "Seven days from now I will send rain on the earth for forty days and forty nights, and I will wipe from the face of the earth every living creature I have made" (v. 4).

Moses recorded that after the animals had come safely into the ark, Noah and his family, consisting of his wife and three sons and their wives, also entered the ark. Now the situation was entirely changed. Everything that preceded the flood was fulfilled. The door to the ark was shut, and then it began to rain. In a similar way, many prophecies have to be fulfilled leading up to the second coming. As the period of the great tribulation progresses, and those who understand the prophecies of the end times realize that approximately three and a half years have passed, they will undoubtedly know and expect Christ to come even though the prophecies are not specifically detailed to allow them to know the day or hour. But such people will know the year.

Later, Jesus compared the flood of Noah to the time of the second coming. He stated,

> That is how it will be at the coming of the Son of Man. Two men will be in the field; one will be taken and the other left. Two women will be grinding with a hand mill; one will be taken and the other left.

> Therefore keep watch, because you do not
> know on what day your Lord will come. (Matt.
> 24:39–42)

The conclusion for those living at the time of the second coming is similar to that reached at the time of Noah: "Keep watch, because you do not know on what day your Lord will come" (v. 42). Though the passage is talking about the second coming of Christ and not the period preceding the rapture, if those living in the period before the second coming—who are able to see signs indicating the approach of the second coming—should be watching, how much more should those waiting for the rapture, which has no signs, live in constant expectation of the imminent return of Jesus for His church.

LIVE WATCHFUL LIVES

> Understand this: If the owner of the house
> had known at what time of night the thief was
> coming, he would have kept watch and would
> not have let his house be broken into. So you
> also must be ready, because the Son of Man will
> come at an hour when you do not expect him.
> (Matt. 24:43–44)

Jesus talked about the watchfulness that would be required of the owner of a house who did not know when a thief would break in (v. 43). Not knowing the exact hour, he would have to watch continuously. Jesus applied this to those waiting for the second coming: "You also must be ready, because the Son of Man will come at an hour when you do not expect him" (v. 44).

BE FAITHFUL WITH YOUR GIFTS

Who then is the faithful and wise servant, whom the master has put in charge of the servants in his household to give them their food at the proper time? It will be good for that servant whose master finds him doing so when he returns. Truly I tell you, he will put him in charge of all his possessions. But suppose that servant is wicked and says to himself, "My master is staying away a long time," and he then begins to beat his fellow servants and to eat and drink with drunkards. The master of that servant will come on a day when he does not expect him and at an hour he is not aware of. (Matt. 24:45–50)

A person who is waiting for the second coming of Christ is like a servant put in charge of his master's house. Not knowing when his master would return, the servant was urged to be faithful (vv. 45–47). If, however, the servant took advantage of his master and abused his fellow servants and lived the life of a drunkard, he would experience the judgment of his master when the master returned unexpectedly (vv. 48–50). Jesus stated that the unfaithful servant would be cut in pieces and placed with the hypocrites (v. 51). The implication of this passage is that belief in the second coming of Christ is linked to belief in His first coming. If one accepts who Christ was and what He did in His first coming, he will also accept who Christ will be and what He will do at His second coming and, accordingly, will live in preparation.

BE PREPARED

> At that time the kingdom of heaven will be like ten virgins who took their lamps and went out to meet the bridegroom. Five of them were foolish and five were wise. The foolish ones took their lamps but did not take any oil with them. The wise ones, however, took oil in jars along with their lamps. The bridegroom was a long time in coming, and they all became drowsy and fell asleep.
>
> At midnight the cry rang out: "Here's the bridegroom! Come out to meet him!"
>
> Then all the virgins woke up and trimmed their lamps. The foolish ones said to the wise, "Give us some of your oil; our lamps are going out."
>
> "No," they replied, "there may not be enough for both us and you. Instead, go to those who sell oil and buy some for yourselves."

But while they were on their way to buy the oil, the bridegroom arrived. The virgins who were ready went in with him to the wedding banquet. And the door was shut.

Later the others also came. "Lord, Lord," they said, "open the door for us!"

But he replied, "Truly I tell you, I don't know you."

Therefore keep watch, because you do not know the day or the hour. (Matt. 25:1–13)

As another illustration of the need for preparedness for the second coming, Christ described a familiar scene in Israel: the bridegroom claiming his bride. The normal procedure was for a wedding to have three stages. First, the parents of the bridegroom would arrange for the marriage with the parents of the bride and pay the dowry. This was the legal marriage. The second stage, which often took place a year or more later, was fulfilled when the bridegroom, accompanied by his friends, would proceed from the home of the bridegroom at midnight and go to the home of the bride and claim her. The bride would know that he was coming, would be ready with her maiden friends, and would join the procession from her home to the home of the bridegroom. The third phase of the traditional wedding was a marriage feast following this, which might take place for days and was illustrated in the wedding at Cana (John 2).

Although the figure of bride and wife is used in more than one application in Scripture, normally Israel is described as the wife of the Lord, already married, and the church is pictured as a bride waiting for the coming of the Bridegroom (2 Cor. 11:2). At the rapture of the church, the Bridegroom will claim His bride and take her to heaven.

The illustration here is in reference to the attendants at the wedding. Each of the ten virgins took a lamp, but only the five wise virgins took oil with their lamps. Though Scripture does not explain the spiritual meaning of these elements, frequently in the Bible the Holy Spirit is described as oil, as illustrated in the lamps burning in the tabernacle and in the temple. When the cry rang out that the bridegroom was coming (Matt. 25:6), the virgins all rose to light their lamps and meet the procession. The foolish virgins, however, had no oil at all, even in their lamps, and their wicks soon burned out. When they requested oil from the wise virgins, they were told to go buy some.

While the foolish virgins were out trying to make their purchase at midnight, which could have been difficult, the five wise virgins went with the procession to the home of the bridegroom, and then the door was shut (v. 10). When the five foolish virgins finally arrived, they were shut out because they were not watching for the coming of the bridegroom and his procession. As in all illustrations, the meaning of the illustration should not be pressed to the point where it becomes a basis for doctrine. In this case, the main objective is clear. When the second coming occurs, it is going to be too late to get ready. Though some have viewed this incident as the rapture of the church, there is really no justification for this because the context is entirely related to the second coming of Christ, and Jesus had not yet revealed any truth concerning the rapture. He could hardly, therefore, expect His disciples to understand an illustration of a truth that had not been revealed.

It is significant also that the bride is not mentioned, only the bridegroom. The ten virgins were not the bride but rather the attendants at the wedding, and this will apply, of course, to those who are waiting for the second coming of Christ. Though the interpretation relates to the second coming, there is an application of this truth to the rapture in the sense that preparedness for the rapture is just as necessary as preparedness for the second coming.

USE WISELY YOUR GIFTS FROM GOD

> His master replied, "Well done, good and faithful servant! You have been faithful with a few things; I will put you in charge of many things. Come and share your master's happiness!" ...
>
> For whoever has will be given more, and they will have an abundance. Whoever does not have, even what they have will be taken from them. (Matt. 25:21, 29)

When Jesus was still in the vicinity of Jericho and on His way to Jerusalem, He used the parable of the ten minas to indicate the need for working while waiting for the return of the Lord

(Luke 19:11–26). Luke recorded how a master gave each of his ten servants a mina and instructed them to invest their minas and use them to their best advantage while he was gone to receive appointment as king. A mina was equivalent to three months' wages. Upon the master's return, one servant had gained ten minas and another five, and both were commended. However, the one who hid the mina and had not done anything with it was condemned by his master because he had not taken advantage of the opportunity of making this money work for his lord.

The account in Matthew of the parable of the bags of gold has the same illustration, somewhat changed, which Jesus used in connection with His Olivet Discourse. In the parable of the bags of gold, the master of the house gave to one servant five bags of gold, another two bags, and another one bag and then left.

The master was gone for a long period of time, but when he returned, he called in his servants to give an account (v. 19). The five-bag man brought in an additional five bags of gold, saying, "Master … you entrusted me with five bags of gold. See, I have gained five more" (v. 20). He was commended by his lord: "Well done, good and faithful servant! You have been faithful with a few things; I will put you in charge of many things. Come and share your master's happiness!" (v. 21). When the two-bag man reported, he, likewise, had doubled his money and received precisely the same commendation (vv. 22–23).

The one-bag man, however, had a different report: "'Master,' he said, 'I knew that you are a hard man, harvesting where you have not sown and gathering where you have not scattered seed.

So I was afraid and went out and hid your gold in the ground. See, here is what belongs to you'" (vv. 24–25).

The master judged his servant, saying, "You wicked, lazy servant! So you knew that I harvest where I have not sown and gather where I have not scattered seed? Well then, you should have put my money on deposit with the bankers, so that when I returned I would have received it back with interest" (vv. 26–27). The handling of the one-bag man is one of the major points of this illustration. Why was the master so hard on his servant? The answer is that the servant indicated he had serious questions as to whether the master would return. If the master did not, the servant could keep the money and not report it as part of his master's estate. If the master returned, he would be able to reproduce the gold and could not be accused of stealing. What the unprofitable servant displayed was lack of faith in his master and a desire to have his master's money illegally.

The point is that those who reject the truth of the return of the Lord are, in effect, nullifying the fact of His first coming, as acceptance of one should lead to acceptance of the other. In the illustration, the master declared,

> Take the bag of gold from him and give it to the one who has ten bags. For whoever has will be given more, and they will have an abundance. Whoever does not have, even what they have will be taken from them. And throw that worthless servant outside, into the darkness, where

there will be weeping and gnashing of teeth.
(vv. 28–30)

As is brought out in 2 Peter 3:3–4, for one to question the literalness of Christ's second coming raises questions as to whether the person believes in the first coming. If Jesus is indeed the Son of God, then His coming again is both reasonable and to be expected. If He is not the Son of God, of course He will not return. Accordingly, a lack of faith in the second coming stems from a lack of faith in the first coming. The one-bag man indicated outward profession of service to his master but did not possess real faith.

STRIVE TO BE BLAMELESS

May God himself, the God of peace, sanctify you
through and through. May your whole spirit,
soul and body be kept blameless at the coming
of our Lord Jesus Christ. The one who calls you
is faithful, and he will do it. (1 Thess. 5:23–24)

In referring to a Christian as having spirit, soul, and body, Paul was recognizing the essential elements of human personality. A Christian has a body, which will die but will be resurrected. He also has a soul, which refers to the psychological aspect of human life, and a spirit, which seems to refer to one's God-consciousness and religious experiences. Though it can be demonstrated in Scripture that all these terms are sometimes used synonymously for an individual and that the whole person is in view, these form the constituent elements of human personality.

This incredible work is one that only God can do. A believer in Christ can be part of the sanctification process by availing himself of the means to sanctification, such as the Word of God, prayer, fellowship with the Lord's people, and study of the Scriptures. In the end, however, God must do the sanctification in order for it to be effective. Paul anticipated the ultimate when all Christians will stand in heaven complete, with new bodies, without sin, blemish, or defilement.

WAIT PATIENTLY FOR THE LORD

> Be patient, then, brothers and sisters, until the Lord's coming. See how the farmer waits for the land to yield its valuable crop, patiently waiting for the autumn and spring rains. You too, be patient and stand firm, because the Lord's coming is near. (James 5:7–8)

A comparison is made between believers waiting for the coming of the Lord and the farmer waiting for his crop to mature. Just as the harvest is certain ahead, so the coming of Christ will climax our earthly work. As James made clear, while we are waiting for the Lord's coming, we should be faithful in enduring suffering and be abundant in our service for the Lord. Especially, we should be engaged in prayer, recognizing that God hears and answers prayer (vv. 13–18).

BE CERTAIN OF YOUR INHERITANCE

> Praise be to the God and Father of our Lord Jesus
> Christ! In his great mercy he has given us new
> birth into a living hope through the resurrec-
> tion of Jesus Christ from the dead, and into an
> inheritance that can never perish, spoil or fade.
> This inheritance is kept in heaven for you, who
> through faith are shielded by God's power until
> the coming of the salvation that is ready to be
> revealed in the last time. (1 Pet. 1:3–5)

In keeping with the "living hope" given "through the resurrection of Jesus Christ" (v. 3), Christians have a future inheritance
that is being kept for them: "and into an inheritance that can never
perish, spoil or fade ... kept in heaven for you" (v. 4). Meanwhile,
as Christians are waiting for their inheritance, God protects them:
"who through faith are shielded by God's power until the coming
of the salvation that is ready to be revealed in the last time" (v. 5).
This inheritance is certain because of God's promise in grace. Peter
went on to say that persecutions and trials in Christ demonstrate
the genuineness of believers' faith.

PERSIST IN PERSECUTION

> In all this you greatly rejoice, though now for a
> little while you may have had to suffer grief in

all kinds of trials. These have come so that the
proven genuineness of your faith—of greater
worth than gold, which perishes even though
refined by fire—may result in praise, glory and
honor when Jesus Christ is revealed. Though
you have not seen him, you love him; and even
though you do not see him now, you believe in
him and are filled with an inexpressible and glorious joy. (1 Pet. 1:6–8)

On the one hand, our inheritance is certain because of God's
promise; on the other hand, it is certain because our faith is demonstrated through persecution: "These have come so that ... your
faith—of greater worth than gold, which perishes even though
refined by fire—may result in praise, glory and honor when Jesus
Christ is revealed" (v. 7). Though persecutions for the time being
prove difficult in any Christian's life, he may be encouraged by the
fact that his faithfulness under these circumstances proves the genuineness of his faith and therefore his right to receive the reward
that will be his in heaven. His persecutions will also be cause for
praising Jesus Christ.

GODLY ANTICIPATION

Dear friends, now we are children of God, and
what we will be has not yet been made known.
But we know that when Christ appears, we shall

> be like him, for we shall see him as he is. All who
> have this hope in him purify themselves, just as
> he is pure. (1 John 3:2–3)

In these verses, John points out the value and significance of being called "children of God." Believers are children once they are baptized into the family of God, but they will not receive their full inheritance until they rejoin Him in heaven. This is a hope that sustains God's children in the midst of the most troubling times.

Scripture makes clear that when we see God face-to-face, we are going to be like Him; that is, we will be without sin and be able to stand comfortably in the presence of the Holy God because Christ will appear to us and we will see His glory (Titus 2:13).

A further incentive is given to Christians to live for Christ now so that their lives will be without criticism when they stand in His presence. The application of this is found in the next verse: "All who have this hope in him purify themselves, just as he is pure" (1 John 3:3).

This passage refers to the present work of sanctification, as *purify* is in the present tense. The whole doctrine of sanctification reveals that Christians should progressively become more like Christ in their lives and that they have the prospect of being perfectly like Him when they see Him.

The elements of sanctification are revealed in Scripture. The indwelling presence of the Holy Spirit is the Christian's guide and teacher. As Christians yield to Christ, they will experience the sanctifying power of the Word of God. The experience of prayer and fellowship with God is also a sanctifying experience. Mingling with other Christians who are serving God also constitutes a work of sanctification. Accordingly, the hope of Christ's appearing is an imminent event that could occur at any time and should spur a Christian to serve the Lord and continue in the process of sanctification in anticipation of the ultimate sanctification in Christ's presence.

O DEATH, WHERE IS THY STING?

What Scripture Says about Dying

Followers of Christ look forward to spending eternity in heaven, but many fear the process involved in leaving their earthly body so they can be given a new, glorified body. Death is an unpleasant—and sometimes terrifying—topic for most people. Naturally, we feel deep sadness at the thought of leaving loved ones behind. We anticipate regrets at not doing all the things we felt we should have done on earth. We may fear the pain and suffering that could accompany the dying process.

Thankfully, God's Word provides a much different perspective from the one we typically hold to. Scripture assures us that death need not be the fearful event we might view it as. In fact, for those confident in their eternal destination, dying can be cause for celebration. Here are encouraging words from God to you:

THE LORD VIEWS DEATH POSITIVELY

Precious in the sight of the LORD
   is the death of his faithful servants.
      (Ps. 116:15)

YOU WILL BE SPARED FROM EVIL

The righteous perish,
   and no one takes it to heart;
the devout are taken away,
   and no one understands
that the righteous are taken away
   to be spared from evil.
Those who walk uprightly
   enter into peace;
   they find rest as they lie in death.
      (Isa. 57:1–2)

THE BIBLE OFTEN LIKENS DEATH TO "FALLING ASLEEP"

After he had said this, [Jesus] went on to tell
them, "Our friend Lazarus has fallen asleep; but I
am going there to wake him up."

His disciples replied, "Lord, if he sleeps, he will get better." Jesus had been speaking of his death, but his disciples thought he meant natural sleep. (John 11:11–13)

YOUR LIFE WILL CONTINUE

Jesus said to her, "Your brother will rise again."

Martha answered, "I know he will rise again in the resurrection at the last day."

Jesus said to her, "I am the resurrection and the life. The one who believes in me will live, even though they die; and whoever lives by believing in me will never die. Do you believe this?" (John 11:23–26)

IN LIFE AND IN DEATH, YOU BELONG TO THE LORD

None of us lives for ourselves alone, and none of us dies for ourselves alone. If we live, we live for the Lord; and if we die, we die for the Lord. So, whether we live or die, we belong to the Lord. For this very reason, Christ died and returned to life so that he might be the Lord of both the dead and the living. (Rom. 14:7–9)

LOOK FORWARD TO YOUR SPIRITUAL BODY

There are also heavenly bodies and there are earthly bodies; but the splendor of the heavenly bodies is one kind, and the splendor of the earthly bodies is another. The sun has one kind of splendor, the moon another and the stars another; and star differs from star in splendor.

So will it be with the resurrection of the dead. The body that is sown is perishable, it is raised imperishable; it is sown in dishonor, it is raised in glory; it is sown in weakness, it is raised in power; it is sown a natural body, it is raised a spiritual body.

If there is a natural body, there is also a spiritual body. (1 Cor. 15:40–44)

VICTORY WINS OUT

When the perishable has been clothed with the imperishable, and the mortal with immortality, then the saying that is written will come true: "Death has been swallowed up in victory."

"Where, O death, is your victory?
    Where, O death, is your sting?"
        (1 Cor. 15:54–55)

YOUR BODY IS A "TENT" BEING TAKEN DOWN

> For we know that if the earthly tent we live in is destroyed, we have a building from God, an eternal house in heaven, not built by human hands. (2 Cor. 5:1)

LEAVING THE BODY MEANS JOINING THE LORD

> We are always confident and know that as long as we are at home in the body we are away from the Lord. For we live by faith, not by sight. We are confident, I say, and would prefer to be away from the body and at home with the Lord. (2 Cor. 5:6–8)

DYING IS A DEPARTURE

> If I am to go on living in the body, this will mean fruitful labor for me. Yet what shall I choose? I do not know! I am torn between the two: I desire to depart and be with Christ, which is better by far; but it is more necessary for you that I remain in the body. (Phil. 1:22–24)

YOUR BODY WILL BE TRANSFORMED

Our citizenship is in heaven. And we eagerly await a Savior from there, the Lord Jesus Christ, who, by the power that enables him to bring everything under his control, will transform our lowly bodies so that they will be like his glorious body. (Phil. 3:20–21)

IN DEATH THERE IS HOPE

Brothers and sisters, we do not want you to be uninformed about those who sleep in death, so that you do not grieve like the rest of mankind, who have no hope. For we believe that Jesus died and rose again, and so we believe that God will bring with Jesus those who have fallen asleep in him. (1 Thess. 4:13–14)

DYING WILL BRING REST

Then I heard a voice from heaven say, "Write this: Blessed are the dead who die in the Lord from now on."

"Yes," says the Spirit, "they will rest from their labor, for their deeds will follow them." (Rev. 14:13)

"BEFORE WE BEGIN" AND CHAPTER 1 FROM ...

END TIMES PROPHECY

Ancient Wisdom for Uncertain Times

JOHN F. WALVOORD

David C Cook
transforming lives together

END TIMES PROPHECY
Published by David C Cook
4050 Lee Vance Drive
Colorado Springs, CO 80918 U.S.A.

David C Cook U.K., Kingsway Communications
Eastbourne, East Sussex BN23 6NT, England

The graphic circle C logo is a registered trademark of David C Cook.

LCCN 2015960922
ISBN 978-1-4347-0991-2
eISBN 978-0-7814-1432-6

The Team: Tim Peterson, Keith Wall, Amy Konyndyk,
Nick Lee, Jack Campbell, Susan Murdock
Cover Design: Jon Middel
Cover Photo: Thinkstock

Printed in the United States of America
First Edition 2016

1 2 3 4 5 6 7 8 9 10

012816

CONTENTS

UNDERSTANDING PROPHECY IN CONTEXT

In the history of the church, the prophetic portions of Scripture have suffered more from inadequate interpretation than any other major theological subject. The reason is that the church turned aside from a normal and literal interpretation of prophecy to one that is nonliteral and subject to the whims of the interpreter. This false approach to interpreting prophecy is contradicted by the fact that many hundreds of prophecies have already been literally fulfilled.

In the first two centuries of the Christian era, the church was predominantly "premillennial," interpreting Scripture to teach that Christ would fulfill the prophecy of His second coming to bring a thousand-year reign on earth before the eternal state began. This was considered normal in orthodox theology. The early interpretation of prophecy was not always cogent and sometimes fanciful, but for the most part, prophecy was treated the same way as other scripture.

At the end of the second century and through the third century, the heretical school of theology at Alexandria, Egypt, advanced the erroneous principle that the Bible should be interpreted in a nonliteral or allegorical sense. In applying this principle to the Scriptures, they subverted all the major doctrines of the faith, including prophecy. The early church emphatically denied the Alexandrian system and to a large extent restored the interpretation of Scripture to its literal, grammatical, historical sense. The problem was that in prophecy there were predictions that had not yet been fulfilled. This made it more difficult to prove that literal fulfillment was true of prophecy. The result was somewhat catastrophic for the idea of a literal interpretation of prophecy, and the church floundered in the area of interpreting future events.

Augustine (AD 354–430) rescued the church from uncertainty as far as nonprophetic Scripture was concerned, but he continued to treat prophecy in a nonliteral way with the purpose of eliminating a millennial kingdom on earth. Strangely, Augustine held to a literal second coming, a literal heaven, and a literal hell, but not to a literal millennium. This arbitrary distinction has never been explained.

Because "amillennialism" (which denies a literal millennial kingdom on earth following the second coming) is essentially negative and hinders literal interpretation of prophecy, there was little progress in this area. The church continued to believe in heaven and hell and purgatory but neglected or dismissed Old Testament passages dealing with Israel in prophecy and the kingdom on earth. Even in the Protestant Reformation, prophecy was not rescued from this hindrance in its interpretation.

Though remnants of the church still advanced the premillennial view, it was not until the nineteenth and twentieth centuries that a serious movement began to restore the literal truth of prophecy. The twentieth century was especially significant in the progress of prophetic interpretation in that many details of prophecy were debated and clarified in a way not previously done.

The importance of prophecy should be evident, even superfi-cially, in examining the Christian faith, since about one-fourth of the Bible was written as prophecy. It is evident that God intended to draw aside the veil of the future and to give some indication of what His plans and purposes were for the human race and for the universe as a whole. The neglect and misinterpretation of Scriptures supporting the premillennial interpretation are now to some extent being corrected.

For Christians, a solid hope for the future is essential. Christianity without a future would not be basic Christianity. In contrast to the beliefs of some other religions, which often paint the future in a forbidding way, Christianity's hope is bright and clear, assuring the Christian that the life to come will be better than the present one. As Paul stated in 2 Corinthians 5:8, "We are confident, I say, and would prefer to be away from the body and at home with the Lord." In the Christian faith, the future is painted as one of bliss and happiness in the presence of the Lord without the ills that are common to this life.

The revelation of prophecy in the Bible serves as important evi-dence that the Scriptures are accurate in their interpretation of the future. Because approximately half of the prophecies of the Bible have already been fulfilled in a literal way, we have a strong intellec-tual basis for assuming that prophecy yet to be fulfilled will likewise have a literal fulfillment. At the same time, we can rightly conclude that the Bible is inspired of the Holy Spirit and that prophecy is indeed a revelation by God for that which is certain to come.

Scriptural prophecy, properly interpreted, also provides a guide-line for establishing the value of human conduct and the things that pertain to this life. For Christians, the ultimate question is whether

God considers what we are doing of value, in contrast to the world's system of values, which is largely materialistic.

Prophecy also provides a guide to the meaning of history. Though philosophers will continue to debate a philosophy of history, the Bible indicates that history is the unfolding of God's plan and purpose for revealing Himself and manifesting His love. In the Christian faith, history reaches its climax in God's plan for the future in which the earth in its present situation will be destroyed and a new earth will be created. A proper interpretation of prophecy serves to support and enhance all other areas of theology, and without a proper interpretation of prophecy, all other areas to some extent become incomplete revelation.

In attempting to accurately communicate the meaning of Scripture, prophecy serves to bring light and understanding to many aspects of our present life as well as our future hope. In an effort to understand and interpret prophecy correctly as a justifiable theological exercise, it is necessary to establish a proper base for interpretation.

AN END TIMES TIMELINE

Because there is so much confusion and disagreement about the end times, even among Christians, this chapter is meant to serve as an overview—a timeline that will help you visualize the major events of unfulfilled prophecy. In this chapter, you will see summaries of occurrences from the rapture through Christ's final judgment and the beginning of the eternal heavenly reign. Each of these events will be dealt with at more length throughout the rest of the book.

1. Rapture of the Church (1 Cor. 15:51–58; 1 Thess. 4:13–18)

The first concrete event of the end times is the rapture, the moment when Jesus Christ takes up all believers to be with Him in heaven, before the turmoil and persecution of the tribulation begins.

> Brothers and sisters, we do not want you to be uninformed about those who sleep in death, so that you do not grieve like the rest of mankind, who have no hope.... For the Lord himself will come down from heaven, with a loud command, with the voice of the archangel and with the trumpet call of

> God, and the dead in Christ will rise first. After
> that, we who are still alive and are left will be caught
> up together with them in the clouds to meet the
> Lord in the air. And so we will be with the Lord
> forever. (1 Thess. 4:13, 16–17)

This revelation was introduced as truth that is "according to the Lord's word" (v. 15), given to the apostle Paul by special revelation. Though Jesus introduced the doctrine of the rapture in John 14:1–3, there was no exposition of it while He was still on earth. This revelation, given to Paul to pass on to the Thessalonian church, becomes an important additional message concerning the nature of the rapture.

2. Revival of the Roman Empire; Ten-Nation Confederacy Formed (Dan. 7:7, 24; Rev. 13:1; 17:3, 12–13)

Specific political realities have also been predicted in Scripture. Alliances and wars will happen according to prophecy.

> After that, in my vision at night I looked, and there
> before me was a fourth beast—terrifying and fright-
> ening and very powerful. It had large iron teeth;
> it crushed and devoured its victims and trampled
> underfoot whatever was left. It was different from
> all the former beasts, and it had ten horns....
>
> The ten horns are ten kings who will come
> from this kingdom. After them another king will
> arise, different from the earlier ones. (Dan. 7:7, 24)

In Daniel's vision, the four beasts represented four kingdoms. The fourth kingdom was not named but was historically fulfilled by the Roman Empire. As described in verse 7, it crushed and devoured the countries it conquered. The ten horns represented a future Roman Empire that will reappear in the end times.

3. Rise of the Antichrist: The Middle East Dictator (Dan. 7:8; Rev. 13:1–8)

The leader of this new Roman Empire is also predicted. Daniel's beastly metaphor continues:

> There before me was another horn, a little one, which came up among them; and three of the first horns were uprooted before it. This horn had eyes like the eyes of a human being and a mouth that spoke boastfully. (Dan. 7:8)

The Antichrist will be known by his boastful arrogance and for setting himself up against God's authority.

4. The Seven-Year Peace Treaty with Israel: Consummated Seven Years before the Second Coming of Christ (Dan. 9:27; Rev. 19:11–16)

This Antichrist will deal duplicitously with God's chosen nation, Israel.

> He will confirm a covenant with many for one "seven." In the middle of the "seven" he will put an end to sacrifice and offering. And at the temple he will set up an

abomination that causes desolation, until the end that
is decreed is poured out on him. (Dan. 9:27)

This treaty will initially be seen as a positive mark of this world
ruler's leadership. The leader will be charismatic and popular, hence
his worldwide sway and influence.

5. Establishment of a World Church (Rev. 17:1–15)

The significant events won't be marked only by secular politics. There
will be effects in the religious sphere as well.

One of the seven angels who had the seven bowls
came and said to me, "Come, I will show you the
punishment of the great prostitute, who sits by
many waters." …
    The name written on her forehead was a mystery:
Babylon the Great, the Mother of Prostitutes and of
the Abominations of the Earth. (Rev. 17:1, 5)

Since true believers have already been raptured, those left on
earth merely professed faith in Jesus but were not truly part of the
church invisible. Those who remain—whatever they claim—will
be part of the remnants of a universal "Babylonian" church. This
church will dominate the world politically and religiously up to the
midpoint of the last seven years before Christ's second coming.

6. Russia Springs a Surprise Attack on Israel Four Years before the Second Coming of Christ (Ezek. 38–39)

While the entire tribulation is marked by "wars and rumors of wars," things will now get specific.

> Son of man, set your face against Gog, of the land of Magog, the chief prince of Meshek and Tubal [or Rosh]....
>
> Get ready; be prepared, you and all the hordes gathered about you, and take command of them. After many days you will be called to arms. In future years you will invade a land that has recovered from war, whose people were gathered from many nations to the mountains of Israel, which had long been desolate. They had been brought out from the nations, and now all of them live in safety. (Ezek. 38:2, 7–8)

The ancient princes listed in Ezekiel 38 correspond with modern-day Russia. But there will be an alliance of several groups and nations that suddenly wage war against Israel.

7. Peace Treaty with Israel Broken after Three and a Half Years: Beginning of World Government, World Economic System, World Atheistic Religion, Final Three and a Half Years before the Second Coming of Christ (Dan. 7:23; Rev. 13:5–8, 15–17; 17:16–17)
The Antichrist's predicted and inevitable betrayal of Israel will occur halfway through the seven-year tribulation.

> [The beast] was given power to wage war against God's holy people and to conquer them. And it was

> given authority over every tribe, people, language
> and nation. All inhabitants of the earth will wor-
> ship the beast. (Rev. 13:7–8)

Using the power and alliances that he has built in the preceding three and a half years, the charismatic leader will consolidate his authority over all the nations. His rule will not be limited just to politics; he will take over the economy and religion as well.

8. Many Christians and Jews Who Refused to Worship the World Dictator Are Martyred (Rev. 7:9–17; 13:15)

Throughout this political and military upheaval, some people will be persuaded by the events to worship Christ. These, sadly, who were not believers in time to be raptured, will be persecuted and even killed for following the one true faith instead of the Antichrist's Babylonian religion.

> The second beast was given power to give breath
> to the image of the first beast, so that the image
> could speak and cause all who refused to worship
> the image to be killed. (Rev. 13:15)

9. Catastrophic Divine Judgments Represented by Seals, Trumpets, and Bowls Poured Out on the Earth (Rev. 6–18)

As bad as the tribulation has been up to this point, it still has room to get worse. God will unleash cosmic catastrophes on the entire earth.

> There was a great earthquake. The sun turned black
> like sackcloth made of goat hair, the whole moon
> turned blood red, and the stars in the sky fell to
> earth, as figs drop from a fig tree when shaken by
> a strong wind. The heavens receded like a scroll
> being rolled up, and every mountain and island was
> removed from its place. (Rev. 6:12–14)

The earth will experience physical, geological consequences of God's wrath and judgment.

10. World War Breaks Out Focusing on the Middle East: Battle of Armageddon (Dan. 11:40–45; Rev. 9:13–21; 16:12–16)

While most will quake in fear at the physical destruction around them, the Antichrist will take it as an opportunity to crush all who are not in thrall to him.

> He will invade many countries and sweep through
> them like a flood. He will also invade the Beautiful
> Land. Many countries will fall. (Dan. 11:40–41)

11. Babylon Destroyed (Rev. 18)

For all his plotting, and his political and military might, the Antichrist is still under the sovereign plan of God. All his striving and grasping for authority will ultimately serve only to be the final sign of Jesus Christ's second coming. The capital of his kingdom, the metaphorical Babylon, will be destroyed.

Then a mighty angel picked up a boulder the size of
a large millstone and threw it into the sea, and said:

"With such violence
 the great city of Babylon will be thrown down,
 never to be found again." (Rev. 18:21)

12. Second Coming of Christ (Matt. 24:27–31; Rev. 19:11–21)

Finally! The blessed and awaited event will happen. Christ will come
down in His full power and authority.

Then will appear the sign of the Son of Man in
heaven. And then all the peoples of the earth will
mourn when they see the Son of Man coming on
the clouds of heaven, with power and great glory.
And he will send his angels with a loud trumpet
call, and they will gather his elect from the four
winds, from one end of the heavens to the other.
(Matt. 24:30–31)

The earth will "mourn" because by this time all of Christ's believers will have been either raptured or martyred. The people left on
earth will be those who have rejected Christ. This will lead to the
next event.

13. Judgment of Wicked Jews and Gentiles (Ezek. 20:33–38; Matt. 25:31–46; Jude vv. 14–15; Rev. 19:15–21; 20:1–4)

This is not the ultimate judgment of believers. This is an earthly judgment of the wicked, preliminary to Christ's "great white throne judgment" of the living and the dead.

> See, the Lord is coming with thousands upon thousands of his holy ones to judge everyone, and to convict all of them of all the ungodly acts they have committed in their ungodliness, and of all the defiant words ungodly sinners have spoken against him. (Jude vv. 14–15)

14. Satan Bound for One Thousand Years (Rev. 20:1–3)

When Christ comes at the end of the tribulation, He will judge the living who have survived the catastrophes. He will also judge Satan himself, keeping him out of trouble during Christ's millennial kingdom.

> And I saw an angel coming down out of heaven, having the key to the Abyss and holding in his hand a great chain. He seized the dragon, that ancient serpent, who is the devil, or Satan, and bound him for a thousand years. (Rev. 20:1–2)

15. Resurrection of Tribulation Saints and Old Testament Saints (Dan. 12:2; Rev. 20:4)

With all the wicked (people and demons) out of the way, Christ will now resurrect those faithful who had died before this time.

> Multitudes who sleep in the dust of the earth will
> awake: some to everlasting life, others to shame and
> everlasting contempt. (Dan. 12:2)

16. Millennial Kingdom Begins (Rev. 20:5–6)

Together with Christ, all the resurrected faithful will live and rule with their Lord in God's predicted glorious kingdom. This will be a time of peace, righteousness, and spiritual prosperity for all believers.

> Blessed and holy are those who share in the first res-
> urrection. The second death has no power over them,
> but they will be priests of God and of Christ and will
> reign with him for a thousand years. (Rev. 20:6)

17. Final Rebellion at the End of the Millennium (Rev. 20:7–10)

After one thousand years of peace, Satan will have one final opportunity to work deception on God's people.

> When the thousand years are over, Satan will
> be released from his prison and will go out to
> deceive the nations in the four corners of the
> earth—Gog and Magog—and to gather them for
> battle. (Rev. 20:7–8)

This will be the last earthly battle. And while Satan might think this his final chance for victory, in truth it will only be the final step before Christ's ultimate judgment and the beginning of His eternal reign in heaven.

18. Resurrection and Final Judgment of the Wicked: Great White Throne Judgment (Rev. 20:11–15)

At this time, all beings will be judged—human and demon, believers and unbelievers, living and dead. All will be under the authority of Christ on His heavenly throne.

> Then I saw a great white throne and him who was seated on it. The earth and the heavens fled from his presence, and there was no place for them. And I saw the dead, great and small, standing before the throne, and books were opened. Another book was opened, which is the book of life. The dead were judged according to what they had done as recorded in the books. (Rev. 20:11–12)

This is the last moment for the "old heaven" and the "old earth." All things that have been will now pass away.

19. Eternity Begins: New Heaven, New Earth, New Jerusalem (Rev. 21:1–4)

The eternal life that Jesus promised us will finally begin. And in this new place there will be no sadness or grief.

> Then I saw "a new heaven and a new earth," for the first heaven and the first earth had passed away, and there was no longer any sea. I saw the Holy City, the new Jerusalem, coming down out of heaven from God, prepared as a bride beautifully dressed

for her husband. And I heard a loud voice from the
throne saying, "Look! God's dwelling place is now
among the people, and he will dwell with them.
They will be his people, and God himself will be
with them and be their God." (Rev. 21:1–3)

We will finally be restored to our original, unbroken relationship
with God that we had in the garden of Eden. We will walk with
Him, and we will never be separated from our God again.

As you can see, many significant events transpire. But remember,
these prophecies were meant not to confuse God's believers but to
give us hope and secure knowledge of God's promises. May these
prophecies encourage you as you learn more about them in the pages
ahead.

Bonus Content

CHAPTER 1 FROM ...

EVERY PROPHECY ABOUT JESUS

JOHN F. WALVOORD

David C Cook

transforming lives together

EVERY PROPHECY ABOUT JESUS
Published by David C Cook
4050 Lee Vance Drive
Colorado Springs, CO 80918 U.S.A.

David C Cook U.K., Kingsway Communications
Eastbourne, East Sussex BN23 6NT, England

The graphic circle C logo is a registered trademark of David C Cook.

LCCN 2015960924
ISBN 978-0-7814-1403-6
eISBN 978-1-4347-1013-0

© 2016 John F. Walvoord
Material adapted from *Every Prophecy of the Bible* (formerly titled
Prophecy Knowledge Handbook) © 1990, 2011 John F. Walvoord,
published by David C Cook, ISBN 978-1-4347-0386-6.

The Team: Tim Peterson, Keith Wall, Amy Konyndyk,
Nick Lee, Jack Campbell, Susan Murdock
Cover Design: Jon Middel
Cover Photo: Thinkstock

Printed in the United States of America
First Edition 2016

1 2 3 4 5 6 7 8 9 10

012816

CONTENTS

WHO IS THE MESSIAH?

Each book of Scripture—from Genesis to Revelation, in the Old Testament and New Testament—can be thought of like a part of a map that points to one man: the Messiah. What does God's Word say about the signs of the Messiah? What are the characteristics of the Son of Man? Which events, miracles, and activities would have to take place in order to confirm Jesus as the chosen one?

As we journey through God's Word, a complete portrait of the Messiah will take shape. We hope that you take time to study and absorb these selected prophecies, all of which were confirmed in the person of Jesus Christ. Allow them to edify your faith and draw you closer to Him.

JUDGMENT AND PROMISE OF SALVATION

> And I will put enmity
>   between you and the woman,
>   and between your offspring and hers;
> he will crush your head,
>   and you will strike his heel. (Gen. 3:15)

Genesis 3:14–24 is short, but its impact has sent ripples through every culture, community, family, and individual for the whole of human history. It was fulfilled by the spiritual death of Adam and Eve and their ultimate physical death (vv. 7–24). In fulfilling the prophecy of death, God added other prophecies, including the curse on the serpent (vv. 14–15). God prophesied that Eve would experience pain in childbirth. To Adam, God predicted that the ground would be cursed and Adam would have difficulty raising the food necessary for his continued existence. In the midst of these promises, which enlarged the judgment that had come on mankind because of the entrance of sin, a plan for redemption was also revealed.

In pronouncing the curse on the devil and the serpent, it was prophesied that there would always be enmity between the serpent and the descendants of the woman (v. 15). Referring to one of the woman's descendants (Christ), God said, "He will crush your head." In regard to the judgment on Satan, ensured by the cross of Christ, the prophecy was further enlarged: "You will strike his heel" (v. 15). This referred to the fact that Christ would die, but unlike the effect on Satan, Christ's death would be conquered by resurrection. This was fulfilled in Christ's death and resurrection (Rom. 3:24–25).

PROVISIONS OF THE COVENANT

> I will make you into a great nation,
>   and I will bless you;
> I will make your name great,
>   and you will be a blessing.
> I will bless those who bless you,

> and whoever curses you I will curse;
> and all peoples on earth
>   will be blessed through you. (Gen. 12:2–3)

God, in His goodness, cares for all the needs of His children. There is no need too small to capture His attention. In Genesis 12:1–3, God reveals His caring nature in the story of Abram, who was still in Ur of the Chaldeans.

The covenant with Abram was a major step in divine revelation, indicating that God had set Abram apart. Through Abram's line, God would bring salvation to mankind. Though only eleven chapters were used to trace the whole history of the world prior to Abram, including creation and all the major events that followed, the rest of the book of Genesis was devoted to Abram and his immediate descendants, indicating the importance of this covenant.

The covenant required Abram to leave his country and his people and go to the land that God would show him. The expression "you will be a blessing" (v. 2) could be translated "be a blessing." Abram was essential to God's program of bringing blessing and revelation to the world and ultimately salvation through Jesus Christ. In keeping with Abram's obedience, God made the promises: (1) "I will make you into a great nation"; (2) "I will bless you"; and (3) "I will make your name great" (v. 2).

PROMISE OF A FUTURE FAITHFUL PRIEST

> I will raise up for myself a faithful priest, who will
> do according to what is in my heart and mind. I will

firmly establish his priestly house, and they will min-
ister before my anointed one always. (1 Sam. 2:35)

In 1 Samuel 2:35–36, God made a declaration in contrast to
the unfaithfulness of Hophni and Phinehas, reminding His people
that He was the one who established and removed priests and rulers.
The priesthood was taken away from Abiathar, who had descended
from Eli, and instead was given to Zadok, who was a descendant of
Eleazar, a son of Aaron (1 Kings 2:27, 35). This prophecy, however,
seems to go beyond the immediate line of priests and was partially
fulfilled by Samuel. It ultimately will be fulfilled by Jesus Christ, who
is a priest forever (Ps. 110; Heb. 5:6; Rev. 19:16).

THE FAVOR OF DAVID PASSED DOWN THE GENERATIONS

I will maintain my love to him forever,
and my covenant with him will never fail.
I will establish his line forever,
his throne as long as the heavens endure.
(Ps. 89:28–29)

Psalm 89:19–37 is a testament to how incredible David's story is.
When we first meet David, he is a humble shepherd boy, the youngest in
a family of older, stronger men. Of all the men God could have selected
to lead His people, David was the unlikeliest. Yet David rose to power
and was declared "the most exalted of the kings of the earth" (v. 27). And
God asserted that David's line would live on forever (vv. 28–29).

The people of Israel, however, were warned that if they sinned, God would punish them: "If his sons forsake my law and do not follow my statutes, if they violate my decrees and fail to keep my commands, I will punish their sin with the rod, their iniquity with flogging" (vv. 30–32). In spite of the possibility of Israel's sin, God promised that this would not alter the covenant:

> But I will not take my love from him,
>> nor will I ever betray my faithfulness.
> I will not violate my covenant
>> or alter what my lips have uttered.
> Once for all, I have sworn by my holiness—
>> and I will not lie to David—
> that his line will continue forever
>> and his throne endure before me like the sun;
> it will be established forever like the moon,
>> the faithful witness in the sky. (vv. 33–37)

Confirmation of this Davidic covenant is found in the words of the angel to Mary, announcing that she would be the mother of Jesus:

> Do not be afraid, Mary, for you have found favor with God. And behold, you will conceive in your womb and bring forth a Son, and shall call His name JESUS. He will be great, and will be called the Son of the Highest; and the Lord God will give Him the throne of His father David.

And He will reign over the house of Jacob forever, and of His kingdom there will be no end.
(Luke 1:30–33 NKJV)

In addition to the general promise that Jesus would be Mary's
son, the specific promises were given that He would occupy the
throne of His father David and that His reign and His kingdom
would never end.

MESSIANIC PROPHECY AND THE KINGDOM

Ask me,
> and I will make the nations your inheritance,
> the ends of the earth your possession.
You will break them with a rod of iron;
> you will dash them to pieces like pottery.
>   (Ps. 2:8–9)

Psalm 2 describes God's purpose to establish His Son as King
on Mount Zion. The opening verses prophesy the rebellion of the
world against the Lord. In response, "the One enthroned in heaven
laughs; the Lord scoffs at them" (v. 4). This describes the attitude of
God toward worldly power. In God's prophetic purpose, however,
He rebuked them in anger and terrified them in wrath, saying, "I
have installed my King on Zion, my holy mountain" (v. 6). The Lord
also declared His eternal decree (vv. 7–9), and God the Father was
revealed as saying to the Son, "You are my son; today I have become
your father" (v. 7). This will be fulfilled in the millennium.

Biblical scholars have interpreted this passage in various ways because it refers to the sonship of Christ. The best interpretation is that Jesus Christ has always been a Son in relation to the Father but that the declaration of this was made in time. Some scholars have advanced other views, such as that Christ became the Son by incarnation, by baptism, or by resurrection. The interpretation also relates to the question as to whether Christ was a Son eternally by eternal generation. In John 3:16, God is declared to have given "His only begotten Son" (NKJV). Because the word *begotten* implies beginning in time, it seems a contradiction of eternal sonship.

Probably the best solution is to hold that it refers to Christ's eternal sonship—with the thought of having the life of the Father—without complicating it with the concept of a beginning. Isaiah 9:6 refers to Christ as "a son" who "is given." Because the decree of God that declared Christ a Son is eternal, evidence seems to support the concept that He is eternally His Son but that the revelation of this truth is made in time.

Important to this purpose of God is the fact that He will subdue all things under the Son: "I will make the nations your inheritance, the ends of the earth your possession. You will break them with a rod of iron; you will dash them to pieces like pottery" (Ps. 2:8–9). The fact that Christ will rule as an absolute monarch is supported by other prophecies. Revelation 19:15 declares, "Coming out of his mouth is a sharp sword with which to strike down the nations. 'He will rule them with an iron scepter.'" In interpreting this passage, it is quite clear that Christ did not accomplish this at His first coming and that the premillennial interpretation that He will accomplish this after His second coming fits the prophetic scriptures on this subject. The messianic psalms generally picture Christ on the throne of the Father now awaiting His future triumph, when He will subdue the earth and sit on the throne of David.

In view of this coming judgment, kings and rulers were exhorted to "serve the LORD with fear, and rejoice with trembling. Kiss the Son, lest He be angry, and you perish in the way, when His wrath is kindled but a little. Blessed are all those who put their trust in Him" (Ps. 2:11–12 NKJV).

Early in the book of Psalms, this general theme of the coming King is made a central revelation. In the Davidic covenant, David was declared to be a son of God (2 Sam. 7:14). How much more is the eternal Son of God the rightful King who will reign on the throne of David.

TAKING DAVID'S PATH

> Therefore my heart is glad and my tongue rejoices;
>   my body also will rest secure,
> because you will not abandon me to the realm of
>   the dead,
>   nor will you let your faithful one see decay.
>   (Ps. 16:9–10)

Psalm 16 is considered one of the messianic psalms because Peter quoted verses 8–11 (Acts 2:25–28) and Paul quoted verse 10 at Antioch (Acts 13:35). David expressed his faith that he would not be abandoned to the grave (Ps. 16:10), referring to himself, but he added that God would not "let your faithful one see decay" (v. 10).

This was fulfilled by Christ, as David's body did decay. David would continue in the grave, but in his resurrection he would experience "the path of life" (v. 11).

As used by Peter and Paul, Psalm 16:10 refers to Christ's resurrection and was quoted as proof that the resurrection of Christ was predicted. Others today can enjoy fellowship with God as long as they live and have the assurance that when they die, though their bodies may be placed in the grave, they are subject to future resurrection and meanwhile will enjoy fellowship with God in heaven.

PURSUED BY THE LORD'S GOODNESS

> The LORD is my shepherd, I lack nothing.
>   (Ps. 23:1)

Psalm 23 is not usually included among the messianic psalms, but the role of the Lord as David's shepherd anticipated the role of Christ as the Good Shepherd, who would care for His flock in this present life.

David declared that he lacked nothing (v. 1), that his soul would be restored (v. 3), and that he would "walk through the valley of the shadow of death" without fearing evil (v. 4 NKJV). The Lord's goodness followed him all the days of his life, and he had the hope of dwelling in the house of the Lord forever (vv. 5–6). Psalm 23 parallels the experience of present-age believers, who are nourished and restored spiritually, are led by the Lord in their walk, and are protected by Him in times of danger.

THE COMING SON OF DAVID

> For to us a child is born,
> to us a son is given,
> and the government will be on his
> shoulders.
> And he will be called
> Wonderful Counselor, Mighty God,
> Everlasting Father, Prince of Peace.
> Of the greatness of his government and peace
> there will be no end. (Isa. 9:6–7)

In the short sentences of Isaiah 9:1–7, the hope of the world is restored. This prophecy describes the coming of the Savior and portrays Jesus's birth as a time when a great light would shine (v. 2), declaring it a time of joy and rejoicing (v. 3). This event was depicted as a great victory for Israel (vv. 4–5).

As we saw in Psalm 89, God promised David that his kingdom would go on forever, being fulfilled by the millennial kingdom. God will continue to be sovereign over creation throughout eternity to come.

The prophecy specified that His throne would be David's throne (Isa. 9:7), in fulfillment of the Davidic covenant indicating that this throne, like David's kingdom, would be on earth, not in heaven.

This kingdom will be distinguished as one of justice and righteousness (cf. 11:3–5) and will be realized through the power of God: "The zeal of the LORD Almighty will accomplish this" (9:7).

THE CROWNING OF JOSHUA

> Here is the man whose name is the Branch, and he
> will branch out from his place and build the temple
> of the LORD. It is he who will build the temple of
> the LORD, and he will be clothed with majesty and
> will sit and rule on his throne. And he will be a
> priest on his throne. And there will be harmony
> between the two. (Zech. 6:12–13)

In the revelation in Zechariah 6:9–15, the Lord instructed
Zechariah to take silver and gold from three exiles—Heldai, Tobijah,
and Jedaiah—and with the silver and gold make a crown to be set
on the head of the high priest Joshua, the son of Jozadak (vv. 9–11).

The fact that Joshua the high priest was crowned rather than
Zerubbabel, the governor, indicated that God was guarding against
the idea that Zerubbabel was the fulfillment of God's promise for the
descendant of David to sit on a throne.

In the crowning, Joshua was taken as Israel's representative of the
coming Messiah; and in verses 12–13, the prophecy regarding the
branch and the building of the temple was given.

As Joshua had a relatively minor role in the rebuilding of the
temple, the fulfillment must go on to the Messiah, Jesus Christ, in
His second coming when He will fulfill the prophecy completely and
be both king (Isa. 9:7; Jer. 23:5; Mic. 4:3, 7; Zeph. 3:15; Zech. 14:9)
and priest (Heb. 4:15; 5:6; 7:11–21). A priest of the Levitical order
could not sit on a throne and reign, but Christ will be both king and
priest and will combine the two offices in His person and work.

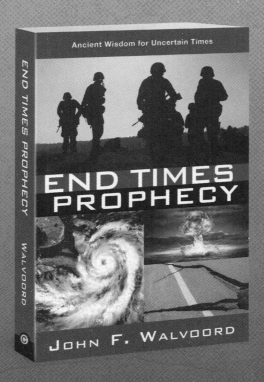

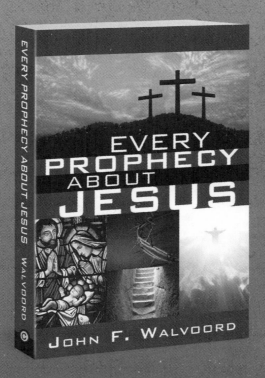